TO PRUSSIA WITH LOVE

TO PRUSSIA WITH LOVE

Summersdale Publishers Ltd
46 West Street
Chichester
West Sussex
PO19 1RP
UK

www.summersdale.com

Printed and bound in Great Britain

ISBN: 978-1-84953-125-2

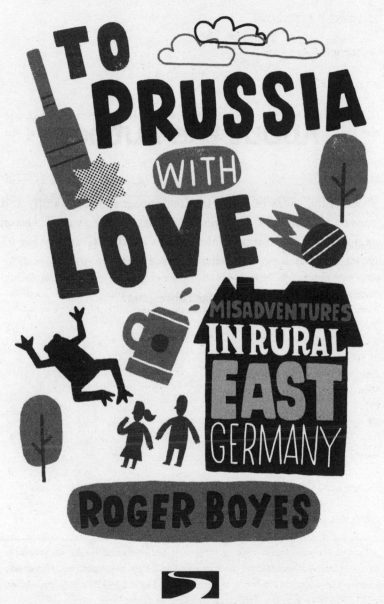

TO PRUSSIA WITH LOVE

WITH

LOVE

MISADVENTURES IN RURAL EAST GERMANY

ROGER BOYES

summersdale

About the Author

Roger Boyes was born in Hereford into a military family and moved around a lot. His previous book, *A Year in the Scheisse*, is published by Summersdale. He has lived in Germany for 17 years and has forgotten where Britain is on the map.

www.rogerboyes.com

Contents

Chapter 1

Dinner Ambush

For an expatriate, New Year's Eve is a troubled occasion. Often you have spent a claustrophobic Christmas at home in Britain confused by how the family seems to have shrunk. Irritated, too, by the fact that your mother still searches through the pockets of your discarded trousers looking for recreational drugs. So on Boxing Day, approximately twelve hours after watching *The Guns of Navarone* for the sixth time and *The Great Escape* for the ninth time, you clear your throat and announce that you are expected at a New Year's Eve party. Back home. 'Home'. Abroad. Your parents make no effort to conceal their relief and you too tread with a spring in your stride as soon as you reach the railway station. Yet once you have arrived at the asylum of choice – and for me this has been Berlin for more years than I can count on an abacus – all the buried questions are dug up, like a dog searching for a bone under a rhododendron bush. How does that Clash song go again: 'Should I stay or should I go now?' Where will I be at the end of the year? With whom? Having achieved what? These were reasonable questions for a man of a certain age, a man who was tired of his profession and increasingly uncertain as to his place in the world. Berlin? Well, Berlin had become a home of sorts but nothing confirmed its alien status, or my own estrangement, more than New Year's Eve. The wrinkled and the sad stayed at home to laugh at an unfunny 1950s television sketch starring Freddie Frinton. The funky twentysomethings sweated in warehouse clubs or in seemingly spontaneous but actually precisely planned parties in apartments with bicycles in the corridor and parquet floors that threatened to give way if more than a dozen people danced at any one time. Over in the west, the burghers of the city – the architects and the playwrights – staged dinner parties in high-ceilinged salons. Twenty minutes before midnight the guests would finish their chocolate mousse and dutifully recite their wishes for the coming year. Sometimes that had entertainment value – a husband, for example, blurting out that his special wish was that his wife would stay faithful in the coming twelve months. Yet none of this ritualised exhibition was really for me and though I had been happy to escape Incredibly Shrinking Britain, I did not relish the evening.

Outside, on the streets of the German capital, New Year's Eve is little better. The city briefly, suddenly, appears to be in the throes of a civil war; 365 days of urban anger concentrated on one evening of dull explosions and flashing lights. The Turkish kids of the battered Neukölln district setting up their rockets in bottles and firing them at other kids on the other side of the street. Smoke rising between buildings. The hiss of a Bengal Tiger hurtling upwards, then briefly pausing and, in a moment of brightness, releasing a green sparkling rain over the city, illuminating faces, flattening them as if they had no history, no problems.

What do you do? You cower under your bed, perhaps. But my dog, Mac, a West Highland terrier with the steely nerves of an organic chicken, was already there. Or you shower, dress up, pay 500 euros, and dance in the New Year. But I dance like a zombie, like someone who has just been freed from a crypt, and should not be seen performing in public.

So when Lena had suggested going out to eat, I didn't complain. I didn't even point out that booking a table for New Year's Eve as far ahead as November was somehow typically German. Lena's understanding of the national rhythm was impeccable; I had come to realise that during our almost two years together, had learned to bite my tongue. On 11 November, St Martin's Day, you eat thick slices of goose with red cabbage and dumplings and begin the long process of fattening yourself up for Christmas. On 12 November, you make arrangements for New Year's Eve; on 13 November you start to plan your summer holiday. It was the German way; nothing was left to chance because that was the road to destruction.

'Good idea,' I had told her, pecking her on the cheek as she rushed out to work.

'I'll book at Borchardt's, maybe they've still got somewhere free.'

'Go for the loo-table.' The so-called Klo-Tisch, the table next to the toilets, was always the last to be booked. 'I love it there.'

'You're so romantic,' she said, grabbing her forgotten BlackBerry that was already flashing like a Geiger counter. 'It will be good to talk again.'

Six weeks seemed a long time to wait for a proper conversation between lovers, but it was only the slightest of exaggerations. At first our affair had seemed boundless, outside time. Then it had been steadily compressed into our working schedules. Lena was an interior decorator and the business was booming. The global economy was floundering but there was a segment of society that had money to spend: the cast-off spouses of Germany's insecure business barons. Lena called them the Desperate DAX Housewives. The DAX was the German equivalent of the FTSE index and since their alimonies were linked to the fortunes of their ex-husbands, they studied the markets more closely than any floor trader. The running costs of DAX wives were more than their precariously wealthy husbands could afford; tax advisers were telling their unhappily married clients to make a pseudo-generous settlement ('Give them one of the unsellable town houses, the snowless ski chalet in Gstaad, the gas-guzzling Cabrio – and get out'). Better, it seemed, than paying the bills for a lifetime of Botox, teeth-whitening, lava stone massages and personal trainers. And what did the DAX wives want as soon as they were ensconced in their new residences? An interior designer who could reshape their habitats ('Lena, darling, make me look independent').

Lena was also doing up a place in Palm Beach and the long-haul commuting was beginning to tell; the woman I had fallen in love with a year ago used to be loose-limbed, at ease with herself; an enthusiast. Now I could see the bags forming under her eyes, hear the tired slur in her voice when taking yet another midnight call from the Palm Beach exile. 'Come back to bed,' I would say, and we would make love, me sleepy, she wound up with her head full of things to do for the following morning. It was no answer; I hated to see her lose her *esprit* in this way. Life was becoming work-eat-sleep. Sleep-time was shrinking, the eating was becoming fattier and faster, and work was making neither of us happier. Our love was under strain.

New Year's Eve was wet and cold but for some reason Lena was not wearing a coat. I could see her through the window of the restaurant lifting her feet high to avoid the icy puddles, like a sheep treading through a disinfectant dip.

'You're on time,' I said, feigning amazement and rubbing her back to get her warm again. In fact, she was ten minutes late but I didn't want to be pedantic. I knew she had been at her office around the corner on Friedrichstrasse, preparing new cost estimates for the property in Florida.

'My stomach drove me here. I could eat a cow.'

'Give them time to take its horns off.'

Lena, hungry, was an unstoppable force. It was her voracity that I liked. Friends, when they heard that we were together, said we were the perfect match. What they meant was that Lena was from Hamburg, and I was from England. Hamburg = wet, dreary, anally retentive, teatime, tweed jackets. England = dreary, tweedy, tea-obsessed, wet, anally retentive. Hamburg = England. *Quod erat demonstrandum.* The two belonged together. I fact I was drawn to Lena because of her un-Hamburgerish qualities. Lena had a drop or two of Italian blood, had a sharp temper, couldn't keep a secret and hated salted herring. When she was hungry, the rumbling from her stomach made her whole body shake and billow like a curtain in the wind. She was as transparent as glass, as untypical a Hamburger as one could hope to find. And the Italian grandmother had given her the tawniness, the speckled-egg look. As we sat down at the Klo-Tisch – I actually did prefer it because every Berlin celebrity with a weak bladder had to pass us sooner or later – she slipped off her jacket. The light growth of hair on her brown arms looked like clinging smoke.

'You're looking good,' I said, meaning it seriously.

'Maybe I look better than I feel.'

'Everybody does.'

'What,' said Lena, 'even Angela Merkel?'

I looked round to see if the chancellor was schnitzelling but she wasn't visible; presumably at home watching television, as usual.

The restaurant was filling up. Borchardt's was, in normal times, a rendezvous for German A-listers, or perhaps the B+ crowd. On New Year's Eve, it seemed we were down to the straight Cs. A starlet was talking loudly on her phone, barking orders to her nanny. An old married couple, with hands glued together. On one side of us, there was a table of six, three generations of a single family. A little boy, maybe seven years old, allowed to stay up late, was picking his nose, licking the snot, rolling it into a ball and flicking it at waiters. His mother, with wire spectacles, pretended not to see this early talent for recycling, on the principle that a silent disgusting child was better than a loudly complaining disgusting child. The grandfather's stomach pushed prosperously against the table.

'If you are seriously hungry enough to eat a cow, you should have the Kobe beef,' I said.

'What's that?'

'Delicious stuff. The Japanese massage the cattle to make them tender, feed them beer.'

'Sounds like Homo Bavaricus.'

'But edible.'

One of my small triumphs in our relationship had been to convert Lena from a lusty vegetarian into a lusty omnivore. I got her to accept the illogicality of eating just green and red foodstuffs.

'You're right,' she conceded after a few weeks of nagging. 'First I was a vegetarian for health reasons, then I got spots and so I became a vegetarian for moral reasons and now I think I just do it to irritate people like you.'

So meat had entered our kitchen again. Lena remained vaguely in favour of animal rights and stayed clear of goose liver pâté and battery chickens and Korean restaurants where the main course smelled suspiciously of fried dog. But Kobe beef, I could see, would appeal to the new Lena. Yes the cow would have to be killed before it reached our plates but not before leading a pleasant life of tipsiness and being rubbed up in the right places.

While we waited for it to arrive, Lena launched into a long diatribe about her customers; their irrational love of gold; the new fad for bay windows; the jacuzzi pools for their poodles. 'If I'm asked to do another leopard-skin bedroom suite, I'll puke,' she fumed, almost strangling our wine bottle. 'I'll tell them I'm vegetarian, even if it's not strictly true.'

I had heard it all before, of course; she loved her profession but not her clients. And I had come to love her, felt a tenderness that I had not known before, yet there was no time or space to let that love expand. She saw me only at the end of the day, or at the end of a journey, when she was too exhausted to develop her feelings, to run them to ground. It was almost as though two hearts were not enough to allow our love to survive. We needed a third heart, an extra ventricle, so that red blood could again course through our relationship. Couples notoriously suffer from the Seven Year Itch. We had the Two Year Twitch: the moment when you ask yourselves, have we arrived yet? Sure, we had weathered the first stage, moving from what appeared to be a fusion of spirits – when we finished each other's sentences and touched each other every few minutes – to a relationship that recognised imperfections. I acknowledged that Lena could be nerve-wracking company if she was in one of her insecure periods; in those moments (which could be forty-eight-hours-at-a-go moments), it was impossible to have a conversation that did not end with a paean to her talents. And then there were the mad times, her transformation into a werewolf if a mealtime was missed or lunch scarcely delayed for an hour. These were ultimately small matters; and no doubt Lena too was still searching for my, let's face it, almost trivial shortcomings. Even taking into account those frictions, our relationship didn't seem to be as brittle as the feuding partnerships of our friends. My best mate Harry – like me a foreign correspondent in Berlin – seemed to be in constant battle with his Bavarian girlfriend, fighting for terrain as if they were pitted against each other (as their great-grandfathers had been) in the muddy trenches of the Somme. Others were plagued by fears of straying partners; or those fears had become real and they were engaged in debate about whether shagging your Slovenian au pair really amounted to relationship-threatening adultery or whether it simply demonstrated over-enthusiastic interest in the family's child-care arrangements.

Compared to our contemporaries, we were doing all right. Lena didn't bang me over the head with a frying pan; I took the rubbish out, unasked. But there was something missing: that third heart. How else to explain the silences on the sofa, the occasional blankness of her gaze?

'You need a joint adventure,' my best friend Harry had told me a few weeks earlier. 'Women need to know whether you are capable of handling stress, whether you will run out if things get tricky. That's what their hormones are telling them: they need to test whether you are a suitable father of their future children. That's why you have to find something to do that is more than just, you know, going to work and arguing about who is going to buy the toilet paper.'

I had thought about this for a few minutes, while Harry had ordered another beer. He was my guru in female matters, my oestrogen analyst, the Clausewitz of the gender war. There were times when he was utterly cynical, and wrong – 'all women are the same when they've washed their faces' – and there were times when he was utterly cynical, and right.

'I suppose we could sail around the world,' I said doubtfully. Thinking: I would get sick.

'You would get sick,' said Harry. 'Why not travel down the Amazon and discover a pygmy tribe?'

I nodded slowly. Thinking: they'll shoot us with poison darts.

'Or monitor global warming together in an Arctic tracking station. They can be quite cosy up there, it's not all igloos.'

Breakfast: whale-meat and baked beans? Lunch: whale-meat and chips? Dinner: whale-meat sushi?

Harry saw me hesitate.

'Oh, work out something for yourself! You must have a dream that can be realised with Lena. Surprise her! Women like to be surprised. You have a bit of time before New Year's Eve. Do some research. And think adventure, not romance – Lena's too bright to be taken in by sentimental goo.'

I liked Borchardt's. It was a barn of a place. Its nineteen-euro Schnitzels were a little too popular with mini-celebrities and their hairdressers, but it had a vague sense of history, a Huguenots meeting place that had later become Hermann Göring's favourite restaurant, a suitable place to muse whether one should prefer guns to butter or butter to guns. Obviously a restaurant for my editor who was fascinated both by Nazis and by truffles. There was something of Nero about my boss; he could, at a whim, destroy the image of a country by refusing to publish anything serious about the place or by proclaiming himself bored. Newspaper editors were the last people in Britain to enjoy imperial privilege.

'You OK?' asked Lena, catching my grimace.

'I was just thinking about my boss.'

'Don't,' she said, leaning over to touch my hand, 'try and concentrate on positive karma. New year, new beginnings, that kind of thing.'

It wasn't so easy though. Some months earlier I had hoped, naively, that my newspaper was going to officially declare the end of World War Two. There was a new boss. The old one, with a face like cracked concrete, had been obsessed with Germany's past. It seemed somehow to be tangled up with Britain's decline. Why had Britain won the war but lost an empire? Why had Germans lost the war but won control over the continent? The publisher had replaced him with a man so young he could have been my illegitimate son. I went to see him in London to bring him the news that Hitler was now well and truly dead.

'Good to see you!' he said, scrambling to remember my name. He wore a beard and so did his three deputies. Sitting in his conference room was like being together with a community of cave-dwellers waiting for the Ice Age to end.

'Online news is the future,' he boomed. We all nodded, the beards and me. 'So we expect our correspondents to generate new readers. Our surveys show that the most popular stories from Germany are...' he glanced down at a piece of paper, '... about polar bears. There are polar bears in Germany?'

He seemed genuinely puzzled.

'Just a few,' I said, 'in zoos. One has become a star.'

The editor stared at me, unsure whether I was being subversive.

'Good,' he said, finally. 'Stick to those bears! The readers love them.'

He went down the list.

'No more Boris Becker, please. But we will take freaks, German freaks; they get a lot of clicks. So: cannibals, babies in deep freezes, incest families.'

I pretended to take notes. 'That was Austria,' I said, 'the incest family. Not Germany.'

The editor rubbed his beard and his three deputies did the same.

'That's what the Germans always say, isn't it? Which reminds me: more Nazis please! Hitler is the darling of the Internet, the all-time favourite; Adolf sells.'

He was right, of course. Britain's unhealthy fascination for Hitler was no longer just a historical oddity. It had become scientific marketing. The Nazis used to shout: One Reich, one people, one Führer! Now, to keep up Internet traffic, we had adapted the slogan to: One click, one Führer. I was in the wrong profession; I should have been a taxidermist, embalming and stuffing old dictators.

'I think I would like to take a sabbatical,' I told the beards. 'Time, you know, to contemplate.'

The editor dug in his ear with a pen, always a sign that he was on edge.

'Are you feeling all right, no health problems? He looks fine, doesn't he?' The editor looked towards his claqueurs. One had picked up a pencil and I waited for him to imitate the boss by sticking it in one of his orifices. 'Yes,' he said, 'for a correspondent, he looks fine.'

'Pleased to hear it,' I said. 'It's probably the last stage before burnout. You know how it is with steaks: rare, medium, well done – and burned to charcoal. I'm at the well-done level. Looking good on the surface but in a few more minutes I'll be inedible.'

The boss exchanged glances with the other beards. As if to say: the man really is on the verge of madness.

'Yes, quite. Well, I suppose we can let you go for a while. But make sure you come back to us refreshed and full of ideas.'

So, rather than risk the breakdown of his Man in Berlin, the editor granted me a six months' unpaid leave of absence, starting on the first of January.

All I had to do was to come up with a project that would somehow enrich my abilities as a foreign correspondent. Like work in a mental hospital. Or a zoo. Lena had been pleased for me but I knew that she was worried that we would drift apart: she with her all-consuming job; me on the run from my nonsensical profession. And I really did not have a concept for my half year off. For the first time in my life I didn't have a plan.

Just as the Kobe steak arrived, delivered to the table with the special care that waiters use when transporting the most expensive dish on the menu, there was some commotion from the neighbouring table. A scraping of chairs; a clearing of throats. Lena smiled gratefully at the waiter and we both leaned to listen in to the chatter coming from the next table. The Germans are a nation of restaurant eavesdroppers; perhaps because of the tendency to cluster tables together and maximise profit; perhaps because of so many decades of Nazi and communist dictatorship that had established a tradition of snooping on your neighbour. Either way, I had come to share the national passion for nosiness. Some of my best journalistic scoops had come from using my ears as radar devices.

The grandfather was tapping on his wine glass with his dessert fork. The table fell silent apart from a low-pitched whistle: the rebellious boy was blowing on the top of an empty Coke bottle.

'Shhh!' His mother snatched the improvised instrument. 'Opa wants to make a speech.'

'I don't want to listen to Opa, he's old.' The mother caught my disapproving glance and smiled apologetically.

'It has been a good year for our family,' announced the grandfather and I could see the various relatives arranging their faces for the long annual review: success in the family business, a silver wedding anniversary, a happy pregnancy, the promotion of a son-in-law. Opa was paying for a night at Borchardt's and tribute had to be paid by the rest of the family.

'I want to go to the toilet,' said the boy.

'Wait,' said his mother.

'And in June,' said Opa, who was soldiering his way through the calendar, 'we had a wonderful time at the Kiel regatta.'

'Wasn't that in July?' asked a son-in-law, perhaps hoping to hurry the speech along a bit.

'Toilet,' said the boy. I wondered if he had Tourette's syndrome.

The grandfather rolled on, imperious, oblivious. 'In August, Emma's garden was blossoming...'

The boy grimaced at me and I grimaced back. The Kobe was growing old on the plate.

'We had a good year too, didn't we?' said Lena, taking up the Opa's leitmotif.

And it had been: a year of learning about each other, satisfying our curiosity. But now, we both knew, something was slipping away.

'Of course we did. Remember driving up, through the vineyards, past Montemare, that little church?' That had been our summer holiday in northern Italy, in search of Lena's distant ancestors who had turned out to be Etruscan grave robbers.

Lena was radiant now, as if she had caught the noon sun, basking in the memory.

'And then the puncture?'

'And how the village idiot tried to chat you up while I was sweating to change the wheel?'

'Do you remember how you said that this was all you wanted: a place in the country alongside the woman you love?'

'Vaguely.' We had got ourselves dirty fixing the car and decided to take a room in the village, to clean up and slow down.

'Of course you do. We talked about how we would really like to live, not in a city choking on fumes. You wanted to throw open the window and hear the singing of larks...'

'Before they got gunned down by Italian hunters.'

'... and the clip-clop of horses' hooves, and get dew on your bare feet...'

'That was your idea. I hate wet feet.'

'... before collecting the fresh eggs for breakfast.'

'I hate eggs for breakfast.'

'That's not true.'

There had been a light holiday-tristesse. A musing about the roads we had chosen, the roads rejected. I had been moaning about my increasingly senseless job as a foreign correspondent. The journalism had started off as a young man's adventure; all my generation at university had been desperate to leave Mrs Thatcher's Britain. Now those years are hailed as an epochal turning point. To us, though, Milk-Snatcher Thatcher, setting her sights on the sloppily financed universities, seemed to be replacing Great Britain with Mean Britain. And we wanted out. Some took refuge in what seemed like Thatcher-resistant institutions – the Foreign Office, the BBC, the British Council – and arranged foreign postings. Others went to teach English and Drama to the bright, bored daughters of rich Greek shipowners, walking to class every morning down the beach; writing notes in the siesta that could one day become the germ of a sardonic novel about Britain's failures. As for me, I set out to report from abroad. It had been a good life: bloody wars and revolutions and absolutely no dinner party conversations about the rising prices of a Georgian attic in Islington. But my other self-exiled contemporaries had made their way back to Britain, many shamefacedly admitting that they might have misjudged Thatcher and that she did not perhaps, on balance, figure alongside Pol Pot and Baby Doc in the Tyrants' Top Ten. I stayed on abroad, and from a safe distance watched Britain change and not-change. Every weekend my now chosen non-home town of Berlin was invaded by whey-faced easyJet clubbers convinced that the city, my refuge, was cool. Or hot. Or whatever. It was never that though. Berlin was merely unfinished, the result of an untidy merger between east and west. Cheap rents meant space for galleries and discotheques and writers. In the end though, it was just noise. Nothing of creative note had been produced in Berlin since David Bowie had a flatshare there in the 1970s and Iggy Pop used to steal his muesli-milk from the fridge. Low-cost living – inevitable in a place with too much space and no jobs – ensured that Berlin's main product was mediocre art daubed by middle-class kids with parental allowances. A painting sold to a colour-blind tourist from Ohio for 600 euros was sufficient to pay for three months' rent. So why try harder, why strive for quality? The city had become the Slackers' Capital of Europe.

As for Lena, she too had come to Berlin thinking it would be a well of fresh ideas. Didn't the best ideas come from friction between like and unlike? Between East and West, the foreign and the native? Yet her cohort of designers spent most of their time gossiping about and spying on each other. Berlin wasn't just not-cool, it was also not-rich. On the road in Italy, Lena made plain that she could do her job anywhere in the world, providing there was an Internet connection and an airport nearby. 'I'm in the colour business,' she had said in the car, 'I match tones. What am I doing in a city that is scruffy and grey and where the sky looks like gravy? I would be exposed to more colour if I locked myself in a washing machine with your pyjamas.' I was slightly taken aback by this image. Lena appeared to be mocking my tangerine orange T-shirts, presents from a Dutch friend. They were my pride and joy and I refused to sleep in anything else. Lena's point though was that our joint energy – that which made us interesting to each other – was being curtailed by the city. In the ambling Italian countryside that had seemed plausible: urban life was turning us into dullards.

'It was stupid talk,' I said, 'embarrassing to think about. Too much sun, too much Chianti.'

'But you wanted a home in the country, right?'

'Well, of course, I did. Just like twelve-year-olds want to win Wimbledon, or seventeen-year-olds want to sleep with Beyoncé, or twenty-three-year-olds want to save the world, or forty-year-olds want to own a Porsche, or fifty-year-olds a facelift – it doesn't mean it's going to happen. In fact maybe it's better that it doesn't happen. Some dreams are toxic.'

I paused. Lena was looking at me with strange intensity, like a Scientologist about to recruit a new member.

'Why are you asking?'

'Because we now own one,' she said, clearly relieved – her face suddenly slack – to have spoken the words.

The Japanese cow suddenly stopped its progress down my throat.

'You're serious?'

She leaned over and took my face in her two hands. So that she could study my face for traces of deceit. Or perhaps to render first aid, since the chunk of meat, value approximately twelve euros, was making me choke.

'Of course I am,' she said. 'It's the German way; serious is sexy.'

Slowly, the drama of the moment sank in. I felt my face crack open into a smile.

'We-have-a-house-in-the-country?'

Lena nodded, solemnly as if taking an oath.

'Where?' I almost shouted, briefly rattling the table. 'No, wait, don't tell me – it's Todi in Umbria, right? Or – no, I know, that old Etruscan settlement! The old manor house, the one with the lemon groves! I knew you had that special look in your eyes!'

The waiter took away the plates so that I wouldn't smash them with my windmilling arms.

'No,' said Lena, 'it's better than that. In some ways. I mean no lemons or anything. It's a bit different…'

'Where?'

'Alt-Globnitz.'

'Alt-Globnitz?' Suddenly I felt cold.

'Alt-Globnitz. It's a really nice place. You will love it.' She didn't sound very confident. 'I've inherited the house from my great-grandmother.'

'Where exactly is Alt – wherever?' I needed a cigarette.

'Brandenburg. East Germany. Don't make that expression.'

What expression? But, of course, I was confused. Hadn't her great-gran been dead for years? Wasn't everybody's great-gran dead?

'It's almost perfect. The village has a cobbled square – a piazza really – and the house was where she lived when she was just married. There's a garden where you could write, and plenty of space, and Berlin is only eighty kilometres away, and it's just very very romantic. Who needs Tuscany? It's just full of sunburned German professors and Social Democrats hiding from their constituents. This is real life, and a dream too.'

'Well, sunburn is probably not a danger in Brandenburg.'

'OK, OK, it's not Italy. But you should see the long straight avenues. Feel the peace of the place. After all the hectic – it's just right.'

Lena reached into her handbag and took out three photographs.

The first showed a large two-storey house, maybe mid-nineteenth century. The ground floor had tall elegant windows hinting at high ceilings inside, and six curving steps led from the front door to what looked like the beginnings of a garden.

'It's very grand,' I said.

'You see! It's a Schloss.'

'No, it isn't. That's what all those impoverished Prussians called their houses so they could make better marriages.'

'Well, a manor house then.'

'Smaller than that, more of a villa.' It didn't look uninteresting but something was wrong. 'This picture, the trees – it was taken in the summer.'

Lena blushed. 'The pictures are a bit old. To be honest it doesn't quite look like that at the moment. It needs a bit of work.'

I raised my eyebrows.

'You know the storms that swept through Brandenburg? They smashed the roof. So we'd have to fix that. And when the spring comes the storks come to nest there.'

I thought about the storms.

'The roof collapsed when the floods came to Brandenburg?'

'Yes.' Lena was a combination of nervousness and enthusiasm. Her breathing was shallow. I hadn't seen her this excited for months.

'That was the year when Schröder put on green rubber boots when he led the campaign to fight the flooding of the Oder river? When he captured the hearts of the East Germans, the Ossis? And won the election?' It was still fresh in my memory: a masterpiece of cynical political positioning by the former German leader.

'I suppose so,' said Lena doubtfully.

'Darling,' I said, 'that was eight years ago. The roof hasn't been touched since?'

Lena shook her head and embarked on the history of the house. It turned out to be a trot through German history. Lena's great-grandmother Elfriede had fallen in love with a minor Prussian aristocrat, a dashing rogue who felt more comfortable on a horse than at a desk. Just before getting into a tank to move eastwards, he made his young wife pregnant. He died somewhere fighting the Russians near Kursk but Elfriede stayed in the house with the baby and a servant for as long as possible before the Red Army arrived on its way to sack Berlin and bury the Third Reich. Rather than hang around and be raped, Elfriede fled to Hamburg. The Russians took everything that could be unscrewed and put it in the back of a truck. After the war, the 'Junker' house was taken over by the state, the DDR. First it housed refugees, then it became an old people's home; after the fall of communism, it was made into a retraining centre for redundant teachers of the Russian language until the roof fell in. Since Lena's family had put in a claim for restitution, no one could be bothered to invest anything in the building. It was, said Lena, with an un-Hanseatic tear rolling down her cheek, a house that had once seen love and was now unloved. The message was clear: she thought that we could bring love to the place and rescue it. She had found her project, our third heart.

All I could think was: who is going to do the work? How can you rest, write – and repair a roof?

Lena took out the second photograph. It showed the house from behind. There seemed to be two wings, built more recently. And a big terrace facing out onto the back garden.

'You see how nice it could look.' I noted the use of the subjunctive tense.

'How many rooms?'

'About fifteen.'

'Fifteen! What are we going to do with so much space?' My dream Tuscan villa would have four rooms, a wine cellar, a library and a kennel for Mac. A man did not need more than that.

'Because that's its magic. I can make one large creative and eating space out of the ground floor. As for the upstairs rooms, I don't know. We can change them. We can do anything we want.'

'Anything you want, you mean.' I couldn't believe that we owned a house – a Schloss for beginners – and Lena hadn't bothered to mention it until now.

'I just thought it would be nice to surprise you on New Year's Eve.'

'Well, you certainly did that.' I kept my own surprise in my jacket pocket. Somehow a Prussian residence, however undesirable, trumped a Labrador puppy. I would have to explain to the Animal Rescue Centre that they should keep their pooch. But what was I supposed to do in a wrecked place in the countryside, deep in the east, surrounded by cabbage fields for company?

Lena pushed over her third photograph. It was just a pool of water. 'It's the pond,' she said proudly. 'The village fire engine has the right to suck water out of it. We'll be part of the Alt-Globnitz community right from the beginning.'

'Looks just like a hippopotamus watering hole to me.'

'Better than that,' said Lena, with the air of someone about to present her trump card, 'it's the biggest frog-mating territory in eastern Brandenburg.' Frogs! My passion!

At that moment we both knew we had to move there. It was almost midnight. An East German pile with frogs that fuck: was this going to be my future? I needed headspace.

'Let's get a cigarette,' I said to Lena. Outside, night had turned to day in the flash of pyromania; there was the smell of cordite; the howl of a police siren. A battery of fireworks roared past us like Katyusha rockets. The journalist in me wanted them to hit Norman Foster's kitschy glass dome and set the Reichstag on fire. Again.

'You don't have a coat,' I said.

'You'll do,' said Lena, and moved in close.

Chapter 2

Truffles versus Gherkins

I have been fascinated by frogs ever since I was a boy, eight, nine years old. My best friend, Stinky Cooper, and I used to take our nets and our empty jam jars to our Sussex village and scoop up tadpoles. They are utterly charmless and for some members of our gang their only useful function was as a way of scaring girls; slimy tadpoles slipped down their collars were guaranteed to produce a satisfying scream. But Stinky and I would scoop our catch into the jars and then transfer the tiny swimming frog larvae with long flat tails to buckets in our gardens. There, we would watch them for hours, waiting for them to turn into frogs. Our most important observation was that the tadpoles which grew legs first tended to be eaten by the others. The lesson was clear for us: it was dangerous to develop too early. Prodigies were doomed to be unhappy. Or to be gobbled up. As we were both remarkably bad at schoolwork, this had something reassuring about it. Then the tadpoles became little frogs and we returned them to the pond, watching them grow fatter and call out for mates. There was another lesson for us: however hideous you looked, females were drawn in by voice. Some years later, our schoolmates – now with Clearasil on their noses and Paco Rabanne aftershave under their armpits – were amazed and envious that the frog-faced French singer Serge Gainsbourg could make such an impact on the sex goddess Jane Birkin that they even sang 'Je t'aime' together. But Stinky and I weren't surprised at all; we knew how it worked.

I had explained all this to Lena soon after meeting her at my father's wedding. My father, who resembled a featherless buzzard rather then a frog, had just married an ancient East Prussian woman, Mechthild Beckenbender. It was a strange match between a former bomber pilot and a former war refugee, both somehow bruised by war, but the marriage seemed to be working. They were safely settled on the Anglo-German island of Majorca, eating pork knuckle, playing bridge and drinking gin. The gin + bridge was of course part of a life-prolonging formula devised by the Queen Mother and other members of the British royal family: the alcohol dulled the senses and improved the circulation; the cards kept your brain working. Lena's father had been Frau Beckenbender's doctor. When Lena was a teenager, Frau Beckenbender had helped her with homework and they had grown fond of each other. It was an odd coincidence: the old woman had also taught me German when I first came to Germany. So naturally Lena and I fell into conversation at the wedding.

'I can't grasp the fact that I have a German stepmother.'

'Why not?' said Lena. 'We're quite good at mothering. We are mummy-talented. You're worried Frau Beckenbender will leave you to cope alone while she goes and enjoys her passionate honeymoon? She's over seventy, and you're…'

'Old enough to cope in a world of disappearing women.'

'Oh dear, that doesn't sound good at all.'

And so after my father and neo-mother had exchanged rings we had exchanged stories. My failed marriage and relentless attempt to find a German bride. Her failed marriage and subsequent attempt to avoid German men. She laughed a lot: a chainsaw laugh that sent people hiding under tables. I liked her so much that I told her about how frogs were made and how they will do anything to return to the pond or lake where they first mated; how frogs were the true romantics, and that was why they had figured in so many fairy tales. Their ugliness matched only by their big hearts and their even more powerful lungs, their majestic croak and their sense of place.

'Do you have a big heart?' asked Lena, letting her dark hair fall over her face. It was in the dying hours of the wedding party, after the catering staff had stolen the last of the food and the flowers; after the last of the drinks had been drunk and the musicians had been paid.

'Of course,' I said, 'why else did I tell you the story?'

And so, inevitably, we kissed, just as the frog is always kissed.

Lena, in other words, had chosen the right way to persuade me that her house was irresistible: a frog pond and an East German Schloss for an ugly prince. But on New Year's Day, in the cold light, it seemed to be a little too much fairy tale for an old cynic like me. Sure, we had once agreed that it would be nice – more than nice, perfect – to live in Tuscany. At core though, I was a city person; hating Berlin, its sloppy ways, yet at the same time entirely dependent on it. Tuscany was an interesting fantasy because I could imagine it becoming an extension of, not an alternative to, urban life. People, friends and business partners, editors and clients, would come to visit; of course they would, because of the region's sheer magnetism, its scent, its colours and its pace. There were whole communities in Italy populated by British, American and German media professionals, designers and architects playing at being winegrowers or simulating concern about their peach harvest, but in fact plugged in to the modern deal-broking world. Ringing up their stockbrokers, emailing New York and meeting each other in the evenings for dinner prepared by an Italian cook, their one point of contact with the host nation. I could imagine that kind of semi-exile: at least my brain would not take on the consistency of overcooked turnips. But Brandenburg? Its face acne-scarred by the pits left by brown coal strip-mining? The rolling hills that were in fact just old slag heaps covered quickly by grass and easy-to-plant dahlias? How could I communicate the sheer wrongness of the idea to Lena, without breaking her heart?

I slid quietly out of bed so as not to wake her. Obviously I needed to think about this clearly, alone.

'Where are you going?' she asked dozily as I headed for the bathroom.

'For a run.'

'You? Run?' She was half awake now, and sat up in bed, her breasts pointing at me, accusingly. 'Don't you always say that if God had intended man to run She would have given us four legs?'

'New Year's Resolution,' I said, 'three kilometres every morning.' I was faintly irritated: did she think I was incapable of change?

'Aha – to the baker's and back.' Lena buried her head under the covers.

As I half-jogged, half-strolled through the debris of the New Year's Eve fireworks – I couldn't go too fast because Mac wouldn't have kept up with the punishing pace – I wondered how I could persuade Lena to take even a modest cheque instead of a house that would end up draining all of our cash. Lena was right in some ways: I had six months free from the newspaper; we both needed a change, to do something creative together. She had no idea, though, as to how incompetent I was in practical matters. Leaving me in a DIY supermarket was like making Stevie Wonder an art critic. Lena would be able to exercise her skills as an interior designer, but what was I supposed to do?

The dog gathered pace as the bread shop came into view. The owner had installed a few stainless steel tables, chained to the bicycle ramp, to give the place what he imagined to be a certain Parisian flair. There, every morning, the pseudo-joggers of Grunewald, Berlin's leafy overpriced suburb, could seek refuge and enjoy their first cigarettes of the day away from the gendarme-like glares of their wives. I had mine with a coffee and a sticky bun which I shared with Mac. A retired banker handed around mints to mask the smell of Marlboros, and we silently nodded at each other. It did not do, in these troubled times, to be seen in deep conversation with financiers.

I had obviously pushed myself too hard because after my first drag I had a heart-squeezing coughing fit. One of the bakery's regulars, a bankrupt property developer who lived two doors away, leant over to pat me on the back; I would have done the same for him. On paper napkins, I started to write down the many reasons why I did not want to settle down in East Germany.

TUSCANY	BRANDENBURG
Tagliatelle con tartuffo	Gherkins
Etruscan tombs	Old Soviet barracks
Close to jet set resorts	Close to German Army cemeteries
Frescoes	Fried sausages
Natural disaster: Poor grape harvest, wine too sugary	Natural disaster: Flooding along the Oder river, thousands homeless

It did not look good. What was I supposed to do in the house? Perhaps I would just end up as its incompetent caretaker; no longer the prisoner of my newspaper, but the prisoner of a building, perpetually sweeping up leaves and waiting for the plumber to arrive. There was an existential question at the heart of Lena's house and it was this: how was I going to spend the rest of my life if I divorced myself from my employer? How would I shape the remaining years? To answer that I would have to dig into my past: had I lived the life that I wanted, made sense of my time? And now here was the point. I could escape those problems, dodge the questions, in Tuscan exile – the sun, the sleepy rhythms, the sensuality of it all. Whereas Brandenburg was, in my experience, about as sensual and as stimulating as a dead sheep.

Still, I was determined to think positive. I owed it to Lena at least to look at the place. And it was always a pleasure to watch frogs. There was more to life than humans.

'I'm back!' I shouted, superfluously, since the door had slammed, Mac had marched noisily into the kitchen searching for food and my phone was ringing. It was Harry. There were really only two of us now covering Germany for the British press. Everyone else had given up or gone into hiding. Harry took care of the tabloids, I serviced my bosses, and that was about it. Harry, in his grizzled forties, operated largely out of a Berlin pub, 'The Pheasants' Corner', which had a useful cross section of the German nation as its clientele. If a British paper had a query about a German legal issue, Harry would call across to a lawyer sipping his third beer and ask for information. At any given time in the afternoon, The Pheasant's Corner would have actors, lock-smiting ex-convicts, struck-off doctors and plumbers propping up the bar, all ready to provide Harry with information. It was, in effect, an alcoholics' news agency and Harry was at its helm. I admired his piratical talent. He always rang early to check whether I had come across any interesting news stories. It was no good telling him that I had withdrawn from the news business for a while; 'You're still in the combat zone,' he would tell me, 'even if you are wearing civilian clothes. You've got to stay alert! There's no sensible existence without twenty-four-hour news, it's what distinguishes us from monkeys.' No time for Harry. I pressed the Ignore button.

'Well, thanks for warning me,' said Lena, 'there was just time to get my lover out of the bathroom window. How was the run?'

She ostentatiously brushed some cake crumbs and cigarette ash from my tracksuit.

'Bracing,' I said. 'You should try it. Not that you need to,' I added hastily.

'No thanks,' she said, taking the last of her home-made macrobiotic muesli from the innards of the fridge. 'I wouldn't be able to keep up with you.'

She strolled from the fridge to the sofa, clutching her breakfast. I liked her walk, which involved a rolling of hips; more of a disco-glide.

'You been thinking about the house?'

I nodded.

'And?' I could see she was nervous.

'I don't like being ambushed. Why couldn't we have talked about this?' I sat down in a high-backed padded chair, my favourite because you could cut yourself off from the rest of the room. It was a mistake. I should have sat on the sofa so that our knees could have touched.

'We never had secrets before,' I continued. 'When did you go to see the house?'

'November. It wasn't a secret, I just wanted to see the place, be sure about it – and then surprise you.'

We didn't really have serious arguments, Lena and I. Perhaps that was a good omen for the house. All I had to do was occasionally stir her sense of guilt and she would end up making space for me. There had been so many other previous relationships that lacked intuition, and that were impervious to prompting. There were times when I knew, with almost mathematical certainty, that I was in love with a woman. And there were times when I was sure that women were in love with me. Somehow these times never seemed to coincide. With Lena though it was different. She had just broken up with a long-term boyfriend and though she had kissed me, her frog, she was still tentative, happy not to move into my apartment but stay on the other side of Berlin. It was, she indicated, to be a holiday romance without the holiday. We would have fun together, laugh together: a sunny-side-up relationship that would end after a month or so on friendly terms. Some men dream of that kind of partnership. It gives them the chance to get drunk with friends or leave their jeans on the floor and the plates in the sink. But it wasn't really for me; I liked having a woman in the house, her subtle, creeping occupation of the bathroom shelves, her scent that somehow neutralised the smell of dog. And Lena, she too quickly realised that we had to live together to establish common rules and common ground. So she came to my flat in Grunewald, allowed me to keep my red velvet sofa recovered from a rubbish skip outside a brothel but forced me to throw out the brown leather armchairs. I feigned outrage but the cold leather was already giving Mac bladder problems; there was no real sadness when they ended up in the Oxfam shop. But however tidy Lena kept the apartment, there was never enough space. And the lighting was too dim for her to draw. The Alt-Globnitz house was, for Lena, an opportunity not only to introduce some more oxygen into our romance but also a place where she could rediscover herself.

I had looked up Alt-Globnitz on the map. It didn't seem to exist. Lena had lent me her supersize magnifying glass that she used to examine fabric samples and stabbed at a spot east of Berlin. Eventually I made out 'A-Globnitz', in cramped lettering. I had thought it was a squashed ant on the map, the relic of a picnic perhaps, but sure enough it was a cartographical presence. Part of the problem was that Brandenburg – the rump of the old Kingdom of Prussia – was such a strange, bulky kind of place. It stretched from tranquil Prignitz in the north, within striking distance of Hamburg, to Lausitz in the south, on the Saxon border. The northern bit was a wooded delight; even the cold war's East–West border had become a haven for foxes, rabbits and deer. The southern chunk had big molar cavities opened up by communist strip-mining. The holes were now being filled with water and converted, in line with some crackpot government job-creation scheme, into seaside landscapes with jet skis, marinas and beach bars decorated with flown-in palms. It was a last desperate expensive attempt to stop the migration of locals in search of a decent living. Somewhere, in the limbo-land between the lush vegetation of the depopulated north and the acidic soil of the over-mined depopulated south, lay Alt-Globnitz.

Perhaps, just perhaps, Lena could find peace there. What could Alt-Globnitz offer me? I wasn't sure. It didn't seem to be the right question.

'I want to make jam in the cellar,' she said, 'I want to learn the cello and just work on projects that really interest me.'

'Ah,' I said, 'the post-nuclear attack scenario.'

'It's just, you know, back to the roots.' She fiddled with her hair; she looked tired. Lena was in her mid thirties, could usually pass for mid twenties. The dance classes and yoga had briefly stopped the ageing process. But in the wrong light and after a hard week she looked her age; the greatest of all female fears, the stuff of nightmares.

'You come from a long tradition of jam-makers?'

'You know what I mean. This global work rhythm has got out of hand. The planes, the instant email replies, the phone calls at midnight. I'm losing a sense of where or what I am.' She spoke slowly, seriously and I began to understand what the Ost-Schloss meant for her.

'Then let's go to the house together and you can convince me that it is the Garden of Eden.'

Lena blushed.

'I can't, I've got to do another Palm Beach trip.'

My jaw dropped.

'You can't be serious!'

'Don't look so bloody glum. It'll be the last part of the job – and I'll be back in a week. Then we can get on with things. Why don't you spy out the place with Harry?'

I thought about this: maybe it was better to go with Harry than with Lena. It would give me time to make up my mind about the house.

'Just make sure that Harry doesn't go Nazi-hunting in Alt-Globnitz. I don't want him scaring the locals.'

Harry had other things on his mind when I met him a day later.

'We're going to keep this short, right?' he said. 'I don't like travelling into the bush in your wreck of a car.'

Harry's Mercedes was in the workshop being finely tuned for another expedition into the German hinterland. Which was a pity because the car might have made a Brandenburg safari more palatable. There was no better way to travel east: behind smoked-glass windows, listening to Pink Floyd on a quadraphonic sound system, your back being massaged as thoroughly as that of a Kobe cow. If in doubt, travel in a bubble. Instead we were going in my battered Opel Corsa that I had inherited from a slightly mad ex-girlfriend. After our final argument she had stuffed her clothes and cosmetics into a leather bag and announced: 'I'm leaving the country – don't try and follow me!' Later, having indeed failed to follow her to the airport, I found the keys to her Opel and adopted the sad, orphaned vehicle.

Harry was stacking a crate of mineral water into the back of the Opel. There were blankets, two sleeping bags, an emergency flare, groundsheet, firelighters, tins of condensed milk and baked beans.

'You've forgotten the shotgun,' I said, 'and a steel animal trap.'

'But I've got a mosquito net,' he said proudly, holding up a brand new net displaying the shop label, Tropical Adventures. We both knew, of course, that mosquitoes tended to lie low in a Brandenburg January but I guessed the reason for Harry's caution. Our newspapers had sent us the previous autumn on a ten-day 'war-zone' training course in the Welsh borderlands; insurance companies had made the course a condition for covering the lives and limbs of correspondents abroad, even those stationed, as we were, in a country that had not seen much war for the past sixty-five years. The instructors, all hardened raw-meat-eating ex-soldiers who looked as if they would rather be night-parachuting into enemy terrain than spoon-feeding baby-skinned reporters, told us the three main causes of death of war correspondents. Not bullets and bombs, but: 1. bad driving in bad car; 2. using the toilet on a long-haul air flight – the most scientifically interesting but fatal viruses got passed on in the loo; and 3. mosquito bites. Ever since taking the course Harry had been terrified of mosquitoes; every trip out of Berlin became a venture into the jungle. And he insisted on driving the Opel; I was to read the map and give due warning if it looked as if we were about to be ambushed by cannibals.

The drive out of Berlin was as ponderous as a funeral cortège. It was Friday noon, the moment when Berliners start their weekend, and the Great Escape had begun. The city was eight times larger than Paris and much emptier. Down Frankfurter Allee, now filled with the smart and young who thought it cool to live in Stalinist apartments, a sharp wind was funnelled between the buildings, making a whooshing noise past the Opel's imperfect windows. A chill slipped into the car. Harry shuddered and clearly yearned for his Mercedes 500. The street was drained of colour, its pointlessly oversized houses parchment-yellow, the waxy complexion of someone who has just left prison. A splash of DDR-red, 'Long live the Success of Marxism-Leninism!', something gigantic and striking, would have done the Allee good. Instead it was little more than a concrete canyon. It was followed by housing estates, built in the last years of socialism and showing their age. Then came urban wasteland, the kiosks where drunks could pick up their late-night booze, the car repair workshops, the One Euro shops, the warehouses, ever onwards until the mess of the suburbs faded into the mess of a scruffy countryside of collective farmland that had been run like factories and then abandoned. As the buildings became smaller, the light became brighter, an unusual winter dazzle. Then, the countryside proper: the Potemkin villages, with flower tubs in the main street, the wooden windows freshly painted as if in readiness for a state visit, and, in stolen glimpses, the wreckage of a car or a dumped refrigerator, supposed to be hidden from view. Seabirds, far from home, and big fat crows flapped away from a lake, driven from the water by a dog with attention deficit disorder. Every few kilometres or so there would be a shrine on the roadside, the picture of a teenager, a wreath. A victim of the Brandenburg chicken game: his foot jammed hard on the pedal of a car with hot-rodded engine hurtling down the country lanes towards another crazed driver. The first to give way lost the game. If neither blinked, the cars crashed. The options were lose and live, win and live, or both drivers die and win.

'They must have some other form of entertainment,' mused Harry as we passed another shrine. The straighter the road, the greater the number of shrines. 'I really think it's a bad idea.'

'Me too, obviously. Such a waste of young men. They could be in uniform, killing the Taliban.'

'No, I wasn't talking about the kids. Chicken's an OK game, we used to play it with knives in my day.' He pointed to a faint scar on the right side of his face. 'I meant you moving to Brandenburg. What the hell are you going to do out here?'

Harry did not approve, I knew that. Not because of any prejudice against the east. He just thought it was wrong to disengage from journalism. For Harry, journalism had meant social improvement, a way of extracting himself from a working-class family – his mother was a supermarket cashier, his father had run away with a younger woman – and a kind of fame. Others in his school had wanted to be football players or punk rockers or bank robbers, but a friendly schoolteacher had recognised that he understood word order – subject-verb-object – and had steered him towards the local newspaper. After Harry jettisoned his knowledge of grammar, he was taken up by the tabloid newspapers and, for a few years, had been a star. Thanks to journalism, he dressed in well-tailored clothes, had travelled the globe (often in search of surviving Nazis) and slurped fine wines at someone else's expense. Journalism had turned him into the simulacrum of an English gentleman. To turn away from journalism, to declare that it was betraying its noble roots by becoming part of the entertainment business, that was too much for Harry. As far as he was concerned, journalism was like the priesthood: you stayed in it until you died or you were thrown out for paedophilia. And, he told me, we were in a business that gave us the freedom to be fools, to jump from one social situation to another – interviewing a minister's discarded lover on a Monday and reporting the effects of a train crash on a Tuesday. It was, he said, staring at me pointedly, the only sensible profession for a person with butterfly levels of concentration.

Settling in Brandenburg was the very negation of my previous freedom. I was, he said, trying to put down roots in a strange country.

'I'd have told you the same if you were going to set up home on the Costa del Sol, or buy a chateau in the Loire. Although at least you could get pleasantly drunk in France.'

'Brandenburg has wine too.' If the world became one degree hotter, East Germany would become the new Burgundy; it was something to look forward to.

The fields were barren. January was no time to visit the countryside. I wanted the soil to be blossoming yellow with rapeseed, or even with wild poppy; I longed for the scent of freshly mown hay. Anything, really, to convince Harry that I wasn't being a fool. According to my map we were approaching Erkner. The German writer Gerhard Hauptmann had set one of his stories there. As I recalled, the hero lost his son in a train accident, killed his wife, slit the throat of his baby; lost his mind, was confined to a lunatic asylum in Berlin. I decided not to mention this uplifting story to Harry.

'You're doing this out of love?' asked Harry.

'Maybe,' I said, 'but so what?'

Perhaps that was what irritated Harry most; a woman intruding on a male bond. We had been on plenty of stories together, Harry and I, and our partnership was akin to the two cops in Germany's Sunday evening TV cop show, *Tatort*: one of us was impulsive, the other a careful detective, but together we were a team defying the bureaucratic small-mindedness of our society, righting wrongs, the defenders of the weak. In *Tatort*, as in life, the only thing that disturbed this winning formula was if one of the cops fell in love with a woman. In *Tatort* the dramatic tension was usually resolved by the woman getting a bullet in her head. I had decided that this was not an option for Lena, and Harry felt a bit jilted. So his question was legitimate. Was I embarking on the Brandenburg adventure (merely) out of love? I was sure that my relationship with Lena had become pretty solid over the past twelve months; the central problem, it seemed, was the role of work in our lives; too invasive, too draining of energy. But I was beginning to understand that women wanted more from me; they had left me in the past because I was so reluctant to commit myself. Now I could change that pattern by setting up a home. My brain was still with Harry: rebuilding a house in a godforsaken part of Europe was an act of clinical derangement since nothing in my life suggested that I could make a success out of it. My heart, though, was with Lena.

Harry interrupted my train of thought.

'Got to stop for a pee,' he said. We drew up to the side of the road. It was more of a lane, lined by hawthorn bushes. There was a narrow gap so we pushed our way through into a potato field that rose up into a gentle hill. While Harry attended to his needs, sighing loudly, I climbed up the hill to try and get reception for my mobile phone. Brandenburg's marketing slogan could be: 'No network available'. Frustrated, I punched the buttons that should have connected me to Lena. Nothing happened.

'Shit,' I said.

'Take a look at that!' said Harry as he panted up the slope to join me. 'What a great view.' I glanced up from the phone. Laid out below us was a patchwork of fields, a copse of birch trees, a plantation of fir trees, grown for Christmas but evidently unsold because of the recession. A narrow stream curled through the fields.

'Just like England,' said Harry, and there was no greater compliment. 'Apart from that camp watchtower.'

'It's a raised hunter's hide,' I said, 'they shoot rabbits.'

Harry, I could see, wasn't convinced.

'What's that down there?' he asked, squinting into the middle distance.

'If we're not lost, then it can only be one thing – the church tower of Alt-Globnitz.'

'Looks pretty.'

And it was.

Harry's mood improved in the final stretch of the drive. The countryside had captivated him and as his enthusiasm grew, so it infected me. We had left the greyness of Berlin in search of colour and though there wasn't a Mediterranean explosion of bougainvillea and azure skies, the winter sun lit up the subtle greens and browns. For the most part our route had been flat and devoid of humans. Now the terrain was rolling a bit –

'Perfect artillery country!' was Harry's verdict – we felt, rather than saw, the proximity of the Oder river.

'Welcome to Alt-Globnitz,' said the sign at the fringe of the village, optimistically circled by the stars of the European Union. 'Twinned with Dunkirk, Hastings...'

'Notice anything about that sign?' asked Harry.

'I was concentrating on the map, the Schloss must be somewhere close.'

'All places where the English were defeated in battle,' said Harry. 'You're going to have a great time here.'

The Schloss wasn't marked but it proved to be easy to find: it was next to the church. Brandenburg towns are easy to decode. Under communist rule, landowners and private craftsmen were seen as class enemies. So they were pushed out. Instead, some kind of factory was usually built to convert peasants into workers. High-rise buildings were slapped up quickly to barrack them. The historic town centre – usually no more than two or three streets of neglected houses – was thus always hidden from view as you approached the place; anything remotely beautiful or interesting was tucked behind a wall of prematurely ageing prefabs. And so it was with Alt-Globnitz. But the church steeple peeped up from between the three or four 1970s housing blocks and we negotiated our way around a needless one-way system until we came to the graveyard. Burying the dead seemed to be the main focus of spiritual activity in Alt-Globnitz. The church, angular and graceless, was locked. But across the low red-brick cemetery wall we could make out, through a screen of trees, what seemed to be Lena's family estate. We reversed the Opel out of the church grounds and found a wrought iron gate marked simply 'Das

Schloss' as if it were a prop in a Hammer horror film. No cloaked vampires jumped out at us, however, as we bumped the car down the gravel driveway, flanked by solid oak and chestnut trees.

'I don't see the frogs,' I said.

'For goodness' sake, just concentrate on the house,' said Harry, 'the frogs can wait.'

We got out, stretched our backs, and looked up. Sure enough, as I had suspected, the house was in worse shape than in Lena's pictures. The hole in the roof was man-sized: broad enough to accommodate a sumo wrestler. The drainpipes were blocked by leaves, suggesting that the place hadn't been touched since the autumn. Or perhaps the autumn of the previous year. The window paint was flaking as if inflicted with some rare skin disease. One of the panes was cracked, the entrance steps were chipped. Two rusting padlocks kept the front door closed. A cat galloped past us as if someone had tied a firework to its tail.

'Amazing what you can do with Photoshop,' said Harry, rattling the front door. 'Wouldn't have recognised the place from your pictures.'

The stench of old rubbish sacks wafted out of the house. I spotted a big brown damp patch, the shape of Australia, spreading out on the first floor, tucked underneath some ivy.

'I'm going to see if we can get in through the back door,' said Harry.

'I'll try and find the caretaker.' In fact, I was curious about the frogs and wanted to find the pond. I guessed it was behind a cluster of trees to the left of the house. The grounds were much larger than usual for a Prussian mansion. I took another look at the façade of the house, trying to see beyond its obvious flaws. There was a kind of neglected grandeur there; the house had survived war and dictatorship and it deserved a bit of attention. I heard a crack as sharp as a sniper's bullet and wheeled round, following the sound. Hidden behind a cluster of conifers, I spotted a small fire made up of old branches that kept shifting and spitting. Stoking it was a wiry man in his late fifties, as trim and as undernourished as a jockey. He had the long face of a Norseman, extended by a goatee beard.

'You must be Frau Berger's young man,' he said, 'I'm Lutz.'

Lena had told me about Lutz: a former sailor in the DDR merchant navy, he had come back to Alt-Globnitz after the fall of communism and survived on carpentry and odd jobs. The town hall paid him to keep an eye on the Schloss to ensure that it did not collapse into an exhausted heap.

'Nice to meet you,' I said. 'So that's the pond.' In front of us stretched a bottle-green brackish expanse of water, as long as an Olympic swimming pool. Just beyond it there was the wall dividing the estate from the graveyard. The pond was ringed by trees and slightly sunken, explaining why we had not spotted it when we drove up. For the non-initiated the pond was not much to look at. There was a small jetty, with a canoe moored to one of its supports, but it was difficult to imagine the boat's function: the water was too dirty, the pond too narrow to serve any recreational purpose.

'Don't say you want to turn it into a swimming pool,' said Lutz, following, and misunderstanding my gaze.

'It's perfect as it is,' I said.

Lutz understood.

'You like frogs!'

'They're the creatures of the future,' I said.

Lutz shook my hand enthusiastically.

'A man after my own heart. One day soon all the world will be underwater and we'll become amphibian again, you'll see, and then every year will be the Year of the Frog.'

Behind us we could hear Harry knocking on a window; he was inside, displaying yet again his talent as a cat burglar.

'He did it right,' said Lutz. 'You have to use one of the French windows in the back.'

We walked away from the pond round the side of the house to the back garden. Lutz gave me a potted lecture as to how the von Pandow family – Lena's ancestors – had moved to the area only in the nineteenth century. The family did not have ancient roots in this part of Prussia – and so the house wasn't really loved as it should be loved. Hermann Göring, among his many other titles also Hitler's Chief Forester, used it once as a base for a hunting trip and there was a photograph somewhere in the village museum of a pile of slaughtered wild boar laid out in front of the house. The hunters were all wearing swastikas.

We had reached the back of the house. There was a non-functioning fountain with eight open-mouthed fish at its centre. No doubt in happier times water spewed out of them. And there was a sundial. No doubt the sun would shine again. Lutz showed me how to reach inside the French window and undo a latch; Harry of course had instinctively understood. If anything the house was more impressive from behind than from the front. The garden was just scrubland, but there was a lot of it, perhaps 150 metres. The tall windows opened up onto a terrace.

'It could be good in the summer,' said Lutz. 'See those trees on the fringe of the garden? They're pear trees, planted in the nineteenth century to compete with the von Ribbecks in the Havelland. You know the Fontane poem about the Ribbeck who gives pears to the village children?'

I looked blank. A former sailor was going to quote Fontane at me?

'My mother taught it to me. We didn't do it at school of course. It's about a kind-hearted aristocrat, and so obviously the commies did not teach it at school. Aristos were the Class Enemy – and their houses were either bulldozed or used to house old people or nutters. So no money was ever invested in manor houses. That's why yours is such a mess.'

We were inside now, in a long salon that had been split in two by an artificial wall. Lutz was still talking but I tried to switch off and concentrate on the space. It had become clear to me after only half an hour of acquaintance that Lutz was an autodidact who was determined to share his knowledge. Perhaps it was all those years at sea. They say that westerners are supposed to be the know-it-alls lecturing their colleagues, their wives and their dogs as if life was an eternal classroom. But it seemed that the Ossis too had an urgent need to put strangers straight.

'You'll have to take away that divider-wall, of course,' said Lutz, 'it was put up when the house was used as an old people's home. This was their common room and behind the wall was the kitchen.'

I held up my hand, hoping that Lutz would understand my need for silent communion with the house. In the background, I heard a toilet flush.

'Plumbing seems to be working OK,' said Harry.

'This is Lutz,' I said, 'he's the caretaker.'

Harry stretched out a hand. Lutz, conscious of where Harry had just been, merely raised his palm in greeting.

'What are those?' Harry asked Lutz, pointing at piled-up tables, with inkwells and flip-up tops.

'They're school desks,' said Lutz. 'It was used as a classroom.' Lutz explained to Harry how the house had been used after the Berlin Wall came down to retrain Russian language-teachers. Modern German history is divided into the period before and after the Fall of the Wall; the events of 1989 are known as the 'Wende', the turning point. The house too had gone through its Wende and Harry was fascinated. He had clearly taken a shine to Lutz. That left me free to explore. There was an impressive blue-tiled stove in the corner. Alt-Globnitz's one factory had made the tiles for stoves, glazing them at high temperatures. Sadly such stoves had had their day. Lutz was right about knocking down the wall; the room had to recover its natural length. There were four tall windows on the front side of the room; two sets of French windows opening up onto a terrace on the rear side. The place should have been full of light. Instead it seemed cramped and dark. Green, blistering linoleum on the floor merely added to the impression of a Dickensian orphanage. The kitchen was rudimentary: a long sink, a draining board, a scratched work surface. Everything valuable or useful had been ripped out long ago.

'It's bloody cold here,' grumbled Harry, interrupting a long conversation with Lutz about the bars of Bilbao.

'That's from upstairs,' said Lutz, 'from the roof. Oh, and the boiler's not working. And... be careful!'

The warning was to me. I had started to climb up the rickety wooden staircase to the first floor and made the mistake of thinking the banister would help the ascent. Instead, the banister knob fell off and rolled free. The stairs led to a gallery which overlooked the salon, like the bridge of a ship. A corridor then ran left and right to two separate wings – where the infirm pensioners had been housed.

From the attic I could hear scratching noises. Mice, perhaps, or rats; certainly something alive with claws. After a career in newspapers, I hated rodents of all kinds. Even as a child I had been kept awake by a hamster, bought for me by over-eager parents, chewing the pink *Financial Times* pages that had been placed in his cage. In the end I had quietly got rid of the animal – swapping him with Stinky Cooper for twelve Panini stickers – and told my parents that little Tommy had gone to heaven. They were very impressed by my stoical attitude to death.

'There are nine rooms with sinks in the two wings, and a bathroom at the end of the corridor,' said Lutz. 'In those days, it was three old women in each room.' He shuddered. 'To be honest I don't much like going in them.'

Harry pushed open the door of one of the rooms: empty, apart from an iron-framed bed with springs. Some mould high up on the ceiling; a naked non-energy-saving light bulb.

'Remind you of your boarding school?' smirked Harry. I ignored him.

'What happened to the residents?'

'Most of them are buried in the cemetery.'

The inspection tour lasted another hour. The priorities were clear: the roof had to be propped up and repaired, the old DDR boiler had to be replaced, the windows sealed.

'Can you find a team of workers, Lutz?'

He nodded. One of his most profitable ventures was to convert farm doors – bought in Poland – into interestingly rustic dining tables for the Germans.

'Next time I cross the bridge, I'll ask around. But it will cost – the Poles are not as cheap as they used to be.'

Harry and I glanced at each other. Neither of us had grasped exactly how much money was going to have to be ploughed into the house, just to prevent it from falling down.

'This is going to be like burning a fifty-euro note every thirty minutes for the next two years,' said Harry. 'It would be cheaper to invade Iraq. Again.'

Lutz agreed. 'I think you will have to borrow lots and lots of money.'

'And how are we supposed to pay that back? Lena is going to work less, I'm on the brink of chucking in journalism.'

Harry grimaced.

'Why don't you just go for something smaller, more modern, a little cottage somewhere? Sell the place and use the money? Or,' Harry added leadenly, 'you give up the idea and stay true to journalism. Why pretend to be laird of the manor?'

'It wouldn't work. Lena wants to get back to her roots. And actually' – this just slipped out – 'I like the place. It may look sick but it can be brought back to health.' I surprised myself but it was true – I felt sorry for the old pile. It had probably never been really grand, but it deserved better.

'Yes,' said Lutz – we were sitting on the broad downstairs windowsills since there were no chairs – 'you are right. The house is like an old ship that has been battered by storms. It just needs to recuperate a bit.'

'But there's going to be a cash flow problem.'

We sat silently drinking Scotch out of the emergency flask brought by Harry. Even Lutz held his tongue, a sure indicator of crisis.

'Got it!' said Harry at last, jumping off the sill. 'A British bed and breakfast! The full works: fried eggs, grilled tomatoes, black pudding and baked beans for breakfast. Endless cups of milky tea with sugar. The Union Jack flying in the garden. Mountain bikes so that the visitors can get out during the day and leave you in peace to write your books.'

'Lukewarm beer and egg sandwiches,' chipped in Lutz, recalling no doubt one of his stopovers in Liverpool.

'Laura Ashley quilts in the bedrooms,' said Harry, 'hot water bottles. You'll bring some British culture to Brandenburg, the land that God forgot – you'll be Our Man in the East, a bringer of civilisation.'

'And how is any of that supposed to bring in cash? Is there any evidence at all that the Brits give a toss about Germany?' My experience as a correspondent suggested otherwise. It was difficult to forget the sheer indifference on the faces of my bosses.

'Let me explain how it'll work,' said Harry, his face flushed at the thought of a new, subversive adventure.

And so through a long cold night, Harry and I cooked up our plan.

Chapter 3

A Whiff of Country Air

It was no surprise to learn that Harry's plan hinged on a steady flow of alcohol. The remarkable feature of our long friendship was that Harry always drank three times more than me yet he never showed any sign of intoxication, confusion or fatigue. For him, booze was simply an integral part of our profession, a necessary lubricant to the creative process. 'That's so twentieth century,' I told him. 'Drunks miss deadlines; no editor or publisher touches them nowadays.'

'And what was so wrong with the twentieth century?' demanded Harry, reaching for the Scotch. I sighed.

Still, he had a point: if we were to make Brandenburg attractive for the British visitors, alcohol would have to play a role. It would dull the shock of travelling east of Calais.

'The Schloss,' he said, 'could become an oasis in the Brandenburg sand. A watering hole for thirsty English writers. Not just random guests. You and Lena would pick and choose, always have the right kind of person in your house, stay in control so it's still your home but you take their money.' Harry could be very persuasive while simultaneously being very vague; he had missed, I felt, a promising political career. 'So,' he continued, 'it's a B and B – but more than that. You're not going to make enough money out of giving people fried eggs every morning. You must have an open bar downstairs, with bottled Guinness, ten different kinds of Scotch, and the guests can help themselves – and pay, of course. How do you think hotels make their money? Through the minibars, obviously.'

'Crazy idea,' I mumbled in a brief attempt at protest.

'Exactly!' said Harry. 'A *Schnapsidee*!' using the German word – an idea marinated in booze.

The Harry model was that the first floor of the house would be used to pay for the running of the whole building and give us financial autonomy. Lena would work on her interior design projects from the basement of the house, which we would be able to write off against taxes. Once we had Wi-Fi installed she would have no problem contacting her clients. And I could write the occasional intellectual essay for *Playboy* or *Dogs*. The main cash flow, though, would come from renting out the rooms and allowing our guests to marinate in slightly overpriced but steadily flowing alcohol.

That then determined our renovation priorities: new flooring, the restoration of the downstairs fireplace – the guests had to feel like they were returning from some aristocratic shooting party to a cosy hearth – and a stable, good-looking staircase to encourage them to return to their upstairs rooms, clutching glasses of double malt.

Naturally, none of this was straightforward. There were the remains of a grand fireplace but it had been used in communist times as a storage nook for mops and plastic buckets. The heat for the ground floor came from the more efficient stove; an open fire lost most of its warmth. We needed an optical effect, though, and the stove looked rather forbidding, almost like a small nuclear reactor, like the secret weapon of a mad professor preparing to take over the world. An open fire, by contrast, hypnotised; it crackled and spat and smelled of the forest. We had to have one. Lutz carefully explained what this would entail: 'You need a lined chimney running up the side of the house. You can't use the one that you have – for all I know it's stuffed with skeletons and dead animals. The gas and the smoke has to ventilate.' Lutz looked at me, not for the first time, as if I were an idiot.

I felt a bit sorry for the Schloss during that first week as we – Lutz, Lena and I – started ripping up the floors and taking a pickaxe to the masonry like the teenagers who chipped away at the Berlin Wall. But then I thought: no, the Schloss has seen worse times.

Old houses, like old people, become accustomed to humiliation. The price of survival is that you surrender your dignity. According to local legend – that is, according to Lutz – Napoleon had once used the Schloss, our Schloss, to house his cavalrymen on the way back from Russia. The horses were so exhausted that they were allowed to live downstairs, eating their hay and dropping cannonball-sized excrement on the floor, while the soldiers snored and caroused upstairs. No wonder the Prussians were so keen to help the English defeat the fat little French emperor.

Lena had spent a couple of days measuring the dimensions of the staircase and calculating how much wood would have to be bought. She had a big album of wood samples and stair styles. While Lutz and I had a lunchtime beer and a cheese sandwich she would flick through the pages, scribbling notes. Since this was her profession, I had imagined she would be more decisive. The iron rule of prevarication, of course, states the exact opposite: the more you know about a subject, the more difficult it is to make decisions. So she dithered like a pensioner trying to cross a busy road. The staircase had to capture the eye as soon as you entered the house, she said; it would curl, elegant and languid.

'Like an Arabic letter,' she said, sketching it on her drawing block.

'It will take up too much space,' said Lutz, taking one glance. Lena creased up her features as if she had just caught the whiff of a rotten egg. But Lutz was right: the salon was long, yet too narrow for a spectacular Hollywood staircase.

The first week had been a constant pulling and pushing among all three of us. In between the hard physical work of stripping the floor came the beer-and-tea breaks when we would fight for our competing visions of the Schloss. I tended to give ground to Lena and leave Lutz to lead the resistance. I felt guilty about ambushing her with Harry's and my plan for a B and B. I knew she wanted something else: an ancestral home, a place that would give her roots, to find herself, maybe have children. Not a place full of lurching burping Englishmen making rude jokes about the Germans.

'An open bar?' she said doubtfully, when I raised the issue.

'It's an English country house thing,' I said, trying to make the practice sound more distinguished than it really was. 'Every time you take a drink from the bar, you sign a book. Nobody checks, it's done on the honour system, and at the end you settle up with the butler.'

'We don't have a butler.'

'No, but we will soon have a cash flow problem. Alcohol always makes money.'

'And we'll need a licence.'

'Don't complicate life, please Lena.'

She looked doubtful about the whole concept. I tried to play down Harry's role in its conception since I knew this would make her even more suspicious.

The problem, she said, was not so much the first 'B' – the bed – but the second 'B' – the breakfast.

'You're a useless cook, and I'm not sure I like the idea of bending over a greasy frying pan all day.'

Lena was right about my cooking skills. My mother's idea of a meal at home had been spaghetti with ketchup. She called it the Mediterranean Diet but, of course, it was more like the Kindergarten Menu. It was the best she could do before lying down on the sofa with a drink to recover from all the drinks she had been sipping throughout the day. As a result I had become a restaurant person; that, and not the kitchen, was my natural habitat. I was, if put under pressure to feed a guest, a great improviser, an experimenter. Sadly the result frequently led to food poisoning or, worse, a typically British glacially polite silence. But breakfast, you couldn't mess up breakfast, could you? How difficult was it to open a can of baked beans and throw bacon in a pan?

'I see you as a washing-up person,' said Lena.

'Thanks,' I said, in a pained way.

'We need a cook. Someone cheap obviously.'

'Obviously.'

'But also someone who really knows what he's doing. If we get that straight then perhaps the idea might work.'

I nodded. Lena was moving in the right direction.

'If we get the cooking sorted out then we could become a magnet for Berlin-based English exiles in search of a cholesterol-fix.'

'That's it, good olde-worlde British Fat, fried bread, oozing pork bangers, the works,' I said, leading her on. It was like nudging a horse to jump over a fence. 'If it catches on, the news will spread by word of mouth. We could put an advertisement in the flight magazines of the bargain airlines – the mags they always put next to the sick bags – "the Best British Breakfast east of Windsor Castle".'

'But where are we going to find a cook like that? Cheap and good don't go together unless you have an Italian grandmother.'

Fortunately I had already anticipated this objection: it was the most brilliant part of Harry's master plan. Harry had a sister who was his exact opposite: a Sunday churchgoer whose only addiction was to strong tea with milk and two lumps of sugar and whose idea of a wild night out was playing bingo with her friends. She grew turnips on her allotment and was the salt of the earth. Her son Darren, however, seemed to swim in Harry's gene pool. Darren was seventeen and was constantly getting into trouble with the police. His one passion, apart from setting cars on fire, was for cooking. He had already made pregnant one of his fellow students at catering college.

'Harry says he has real talent,' I said.

Lena looked at me closely to spot any telltale signs of deceit. 'For manslaughter perhaps? Bank robbery?'

'He can cook, that's what counts.'

'Sounds like he flambés Porsches.'

'Let's give him a chance.'

'What exactly did Harry say when he sold you his teenage Al Capone?'

'That the boy needed some country air.'

'Are you sure he didn't actually say: my nephew needs to get out of the country pretty quick?'

'It may have been something like that. Anyway, he's coming soon. So maybe we should get one of the upstairs rooms fixed up for him.'

'First my staircase has to be ready. The present one isn't strong enough to have us trudging up and down with heavy buckets.'

That then was the deal: if I would agree to her extravagant plans for a new staircase, she would accept Darren.

It was a healthy compromise but it fell a bit short of a business plan. Every time we disagreed about the Schloss we patched up the quarrel by spending more. Essentially it boiled down to Lena's ambition. Fair enough, it was her house, her ancestral legacy. But, having finished her Palm Beach job, she still had big-shot decoration ideas in her head. The cracking point of that first week came when we were chucking masonry and rotten woodwork into a giant skip. Still sweating, we stood next to the skip with Lutz, who had so far failed to find a team of workers, drinking lukewarm tea from a flask when Lena announced that Italian sandstone tiles should be put on the ground floor. Wooden parquet, she said, would darken the interior, steal the light. Sandstone! 'Have you any idea what sandstone costs?' I said. Actually, I had no idea myself. I knew though that it was a step too far. This was not the time to transform the Schloss into a Mediterranean-style villa. We needed cosy and cheap. Above all, cheap. I had started my unpaid sabbatical; Lena was winding down her work. Lena was a little taken aback; she had expected me to say 'Yes boss!' Maybe she didn't understand how nervous I was about leading an existence – for the first time since being a student – without a regular income. 'We can always get a loan,' she said. Not without doing the maths, I told her, and so we agreed to talk it over at 'Gundi's', the local pub.

We had been to the pub three times, but had still not infiltrated Alt-Globnitz society. The only people we knew were Lutz, and Doris Bonkerz, the owner of the town's pharmacy. It was impossible to live in the Schloss – having survived the wars of the nineteenth and twentieth centuries, the building was being given its first real exposure to creative destruction – but equally impossible to live in the Hotel zum Markt. On the outside, the hotel – owned by the mayor's extended family – seemed to have some kind of charm: a half-timbered house with a carved wooden door lit up by a gas lantern. Inside though it was a murky brown and beige; surly receptionists humiliated anyone naïve enough to want to be a guest. The décor was reminiscent of a working men's hostel in the Soviet Union; the prices reminiscent of Fifth Avenue, New York. 'I don't want to stay here,' Lena had said firmly. 'It smells of disinfectant.' So when Lutz recommended his former girlfriend Doris Bonkerz's two-room holiday apartment, we gratefully accepted. The ceilings were so low that I had managed to smash the overhead lamp while putting on my jumper. Now we had the problem of finding a replacement UFO-style lamp fixture 'Made in the DDR'. Fortunately Lena had discovered a website where one could still buy not only the lamps but also other cult East German consumer items such as its legendary gaseous beans, and enough rock-hard sandpaper-rough toilet paper from the stocks of an old factory in Heiligenstadt to build a dam next time the Oder river spilled its banks.

I was coming to like the little town of Alt-Globnitz. We had seen it in the winter sun, the light picking out the village's imperfections, its neglected corners, but also the understated elegance of the market square. Five streets radiated out from the old restored marketplace. 'Restored' meant that the older houses had been painted pink and vanilla or, in the case of the town hall, white with a modern Socialist-era fresco of a worker in a pottery, busily glazing tiles for the toiling masses. This tile factory, like the cement works, no longer existed. There was an inner core to Alt-Globnitz which hadn't been too badly bruised by war or socialism, nor by the urban trashing of post-Wende German planners: no C&A; no shopping mall; no multi-storey car park. Now, walking through a thick Sherlock Holmes mist to the pub, we experienced a different kind of Alt-Globnitz; more mysterious at any rate. We barely saw 20 metres ahead of us and were guided by sound: muffled footsteps; a cough; *The Godfather* ringtone of a mobile phone; the squeal of a cat as it jumped on a dustbin.

'You could commit the perfect crime with visibility like this,' I told Lena as she slipped on the moist cobblestones. We had to find the market square, cross to its south-west corner and take another street down to Gundi's. Child's play in the sunshine; a complex safari in fog. The freezing fog, the ice on the pavement and the slight irritability that comes with an empty stomach:

all that made the short walk to Gundi's akin to Amundsen's expedition to the South Pole. Mac was ahead of us, sniffing the air, but he was no husky. So, when we eventually entered the square, we at first hugged its periphery rather than risk getting lost in the middle of it all.

On the days when the sun shone, the square had a certain charm: the neatness of a glue-it-together town used to add reality to a kid's model railway set. There were tubs of flowers criss-crossing the place; only later did I realise they were supposed to block illegal parkers rather than beautify the town. And four bright benches, regularly painted to cover up the graffiti. Someone in Alt-Globnitz was creeping out at night to daub on public buildings. He or she had not been caught but it kept the chief of police busy and kept a cover-up painter fully employed by the town council. Lutz naturally suspected that the graffiti-artist came either from a police family or from that of the painter. Certainly, the protestor seemed to have struck again: as we approached the savings bank, we could make out some large freshly splashed letters on the wall. While Mac pissed against the wall of the bank, we strained through the mist to read the slogan. 'It's in English,' said Lena. The letters were high up, close to the roof on what used to be a blank stretch of wall. No doubt before the war, there had been a large advertisement for Persil washing powder or for Maggi soup. Now, it simply said THE RICH.

'Well, that's uncontroversial,' I said.

'Wait, there's something above it.' Lena stood on her toes. Then jumped up and down, her breasts jogging underneath her tight fleece.

'I've got it,' she said, after a bit of gymnastics. 'It says FUCK.'

'Ah well,' I said, 'I suppose it's better than Fucking the Poor.'

'The graffiti-painter must have used a ladder to get up there,' said Lena.

'And been really determined,' I added.

'The bank manager won't be pleased,' said Lena and then, remembering an earlier conversation at the Schloss: 'Lutz said it will be difficult to convince the manager to lend us money.'

'Why?' I asked. I knew, of course, that banks only lent you money if you could prove you didn't need it. They were intrinsically unreliable institutions.

We were passing the town hall now. A single light burned in a top-floor room, perhaps to give the illusion that the mayor never slept.

'Because of him,' said Lena, pointing at the window. 'The mayor. Apparently the bank manager will be afraid to give cash to a small hotel that competes against the dreadful Hotel zum Markt.'

'But a bed and breakfast isn't a hotel.'

'I know that, you know that, but the Ossis don't.'

Lena was right. West Germans knew about bed and breakfasts because that was where they had stayed as teenagers on school outings to Bournemouth; to them it just seemed like a slice of quaint old England. Usually B and Bs were run by widows, trying to keep up mortgage payments on over-large houses. Some were warm and welcoming hostesses = happy memories. Others were complete bitches, insisting on guests paying extra to use the toilet = horror show. Naturally Lena and I were planning the happy model; not even the very desperate would pay to use our toilets in their current state. But for the East Germans, the Ossis, B and Bs were terra incognita.

Lena grabbed my hand.

'Let's go to the middle of the square.'

'Are you crazy? We would need a lighthouse to find it.'

'Don't be such a fool.'

Tugging me like a Volga boatman, we staggered to the hub of what Lena still stubbornly described as the piazza, our shins grazed by parked bicycles and other obstacles.

'There,' she said, panting a little from the exertion. 'What do you see?'

'Nothing, of course. It's just like being in a steam bath. Only cold.'

'Close your eyes.'

'Why? I can't see anything anyway.'

'It's an experiment – it's what interior decorators do when they come into a client's house.'

'I thought you were supposed to use your eyes.'

'Your inner eye. Now let your memory take over, and your fantasy. What's out there?'

'Well, the bank obviously, we just passed that. The Rathaus.'

'And what else? Come on, describe it.'

'A butcher's shop. Very clean with scrub-down tiles. More meat than there probably was in a week during the bad old days. Outside, wooden gables – it's basically an old house, maybe two hundred years, that still has a reason to live.'

'OK. And next door?'

'Café am Markt. Cosy place with three kinds of cake. Smell of coffee. It's run by Lutz's wife, Anneliese. There are net curtains so you can't see inside. On the shelf behind the cash desk they have packets of DDR coffee – Mocca Fix Gold – as if it's a museum.'

'And outside?'

'Sandy coloured. The café's new, post-Wende, the upper floors look about the same age as the butcher's. Do you think Lutz owns the whole place?'

'You can open your eyes now.'

'Thank God, I thought I was going to fall over. I was beginning to feel like a prisoner in Guantanamo Bay.'

'Do you understand what I was trying to do?'

'Torture me for information? Make me betray Osama bin Laden?'

'No, fool: to make you say out loud that Alt-Globnitz has charm. To see it in an unprejudiced way by not seeing it.'

'OK, you win,' I said. The damp was beginning to corrode my bones. 'The place is not so bad. Can we go to bed now with a hot water bottle?'

Entering Gundi's was the next best thing to being in bed. It radiated the kind of airless warmth that attracts hibernating squirrels and dormice during winter. Lutz had told us it was the secret hub of the village but so far we had not run into the illuminati. But who cared? We were out of the cold, inside a cosy time machine.

The pub had made few concessions to the modern world. A faded photograph of a women's sports team; an asthmatic jukebox. A red and white scarf of Union Berlin had been nailed to the wall, a relic from one of Gundi's former boyfriends, a disco-bouncer from Köpenick. Gundi, in her sixties, was still an attractive woman if your taste was for shot-putters. She was, as she put it, 'big-boned and big-hearted'. The heart was put on generous display with low-cut blouses. The slight shadow of a moustache hinted at her not unlikely past existence as a steroid-gobbling heroine of a DDR junior athletic squad.

'Get out your pocket calculator and your notebook and we'll sort out the finances once and for all,' I said after we had stripped off our coats.

'A drink first, if you please,' said Lena, 'and some hot soup.'

On stiff stork-like legs I walked to the counter and ordered beer and Soljanka, a kind of buckwheat soup.

Three men sitting at the bar watched me silently. I nodded politely to them but stayed focussed on Gundi.

'You don't have to come to the bar,' said Gundi, in her deep nicotine-baritone. 'I'll bring you the menu.' This, even though we both knew that meatballs were the only thing on the menu.

'Sorry,' I said, 'that's the way we do it in England.'

'You, from England?' asked one of the men. Shaven-headed, blue-chinned. He had the bearing of an athlete but then everybody seemed to be stronger and faster than me at the moment.

'Yes,' I said, 'have you been there?'

The man shook his head and concentrated on his beer. Making contact with the locals in Alt-Globnitz was like sending radio signals into outer space. One was never quite sure if they were being received on the correct planet.

'Well, nice talking to you,' I said and took the beers to our table in a corner of the room near a rubber plant. One of the customers, a man with a bull neck, had put Boney M on the jukebox.

'Seems to be Oldies Night,' said Lena.

'Every night is Oldies Night in Alt-Globnitz,' I said.

Lena slurped up her soup like an Oldsmobile guzzling petrol. Then she put the plate to one side and stared at her computer notebook waiting for it to tell us how to make the Schloss profitable.

'Right,' I said, 'I'm going to be brutally honest.'

'Me too,' she said. Somehow I had the feeling that Lena's brand of honesty would be more brutal than mine. 'You first.'

'OK, here goes.' I gulped some air, if the word 'air' really does justice to the special fetid atmosphere of Gundi's. There was a tangy smell hanging on the curtains, a bit like curry, but more like meat that had been left out of the freezer for a few days. I thought back to the chunks of pork in the soup and swallowed again.

'We – by which, in fact, I mean you, but you know what I mean...'

Lena nodded slowly.

'... have owned the Schloss for almost a month and we face: One,' – I held on to my index finger – 'a probable collapse in our cash flow. Two, our most essential worker, in fact our only worker, can't be paid. Three, we don't have any security to offer a bank in order to get a loan...'

'Four' interrupted Lena, getting into the spirit of the occasion, 'our hopes of making this into a business depend on a seventeen-year-old petty crook who says he can cook.'

'But, I was going to say, at least we have faith in the B and B.'

Lena was silent for an uncomfortable amount of time. I was beginning to think that the Soljanka meat really was rotten and that I might have to call an ambulance. How long would it take to get here? The nearest hospital was at least 60 kilometres away. It was foggy. The roads were freezing over.

'We have each other too,' I added quickly, though more out of a sense that she might be on the brink of death, a panic reflex, than any kind of romantic gush.

Lena closed the notebook to demonstrate that we were not going to discuss figures.

'I can't get my head around the B and B,' she said, at last. 'You forgot to mention there's a huge hole in the roof. We can't fix it until we get hold of some money. And we can't have guests living in the house as long as the upper floor is as cosy as a hospital mortuary.'

I tried to butt in but she raised her hand.

'Plus, your idea that hundreds of Englishmen are suddenly going to parachute into Brandenburg – well, it's just wishful thinking. How are we ever going to convince a bank to give us a bridging loan?'

'I know, I know there are a few flaws,' I said. 'OK' – I had seen her sceptical scowl – 'several flaws. We need to make the B and B into more than a business, into a vision, and then it will work. In fact I know just the man who can help sort this out.'

Lena arched her narrow plucked eyebrows.

'Don't ask – all I know is that if anyone can make the Schloss seem credible, it's this man.'

'I trust you,' said Lena. I glanced under the table to see if she was secretly crossing her fingers, but no, they were otherwise engaged, passing on a bit of Soljanka meat to Mac.

A bout of machine-gun-like throat-clearing to my right broke into my musings. It was the shaven-headed man from the bar.

'Could I join you?'

Lena was stunned into silence. It was the first social approach from the locals since we had arrived.

'Sure,' I said, quickly, gently kicking Mac from under the spare chair.

'My name is Bergmann,' he said, 'Horst Bergmann. I run the voluntary fire service.' I remembered the Horch fire engine parked at the start of Gundi's road. The fire engine had been a useful landmark, the bright red glowing through the mist like a beacon.

'Where do you come from in England?' asked Horst. I realised that he must be the same H. Bergmann who had been offering t'ai chi martial arts courses on a leaflet that I had picked up at the baker's.

'London, sort of,' I said. In fact, I had already lived longer in Berlin than I had ever lived in London. My Britain was a virtual country; a collection of shrivelled childhood memories.

'Back in 1973, at the Communist Youth Games I met some people from Liverpool, they were great.' I noticed that he was ignoring Lena.

'Lena comes from Hamburg.'

Horst pretended not to hear.

'Liverpool, I want to go there one day. What's it like? Tell me please.'

'Like Rostock,' I said, and suddenly realised that I might be dashing the man's dreams. 'Rostock with The Beatles.'

'The Beatles, yes, ja. I haff a question,' said Horst, in slow, deliberate English, the kind that you learn from BBC audiotapes after hours of repetition. 'Are you a fan of The Beatles or The Stones?'

The ultimate classification that transcends East and West, poor and rich.

'Stones,' I said. 'Of course.'

'Me too!' Horst almost shouted. 'That is very amazing, no?' He reached out his hand.

'Horst. Call me Horst. Stones-brother.'

'Lena is a Stones fan too, aren't you dear?' I said, kicking her under the table but actually kicking the dog instead. Mac squeaked like a stuck pig.

'Yes, yes,' she said hastily. 'Keith Richards is a great bass guitar player.'

'Lead,' I hissed, 'lead guitarist.'

'Ah, Keith, he's crazy,' said Horst. 'All the English are a bit crazy, no? Your Ossi-queen. You too with your Schloss – you want to make it into Buckingham Palace of Brandenburg?'

'Yes,' I said tersely. Thinking: are we really crazy?

'Do you like our town?' Alt-Globnitz had 8,000 inhabitants. For me that was not much more than a village. For the Alt-Globnitzers, it was a town. And they had a town hall to prove it.

'Very nice,' I said.

'Beautiful,' chipped in Lena.

'Maybe I can help you a bit? You need young workers? I have many boys on the t'ai chi course. They can use their hands, will work for not much money.'

'Thanks,' I said, and meant it. I suddenly realised: we needed a team. We had to move faster – then we wouldn't despair so quickly. 'There's just one thing. We don't have much cash.'

'That's OK,' said Horst, 'you must meet my friends.' He waved at the two other men at the bar. 'Any friend of The Rolling Stones is a friend of ours.'

'This is der Peter,' he said, pointing to an almost violet-faced man in his forties who had appeared to be in dormouse hibernation until now. 'He's the best plumber in town.'

'Pack it in Horst, I'm the only plumber.' He came over and shook our hands, looking deep into the eyes of Lena, as if she were a sink waiting to be unblocked.

'And this,' said Horst standing up, locking his arm in that of Mr Bullneck and tugging him away from the jukebox, 'is der Robert. Robert runs the Sparkasse.'

A supplier of cheap labour, a plumber and a bank manager: they really were the illuminati of Alt-Globnitz.

'Hello,' said Lena, trying to concentrate all of her seductive-power skills into the word as she addressed the Sparkasse boss.

The banker blushed; despite his fitness-studio build, he had a boyish shyness.

'Do you have a euro for the jukebox,' he asked me.

I gave him three, and saw them as an intelligent investment in our poor neglected Schloss.

'Maybe we could have a chat sometime,' I said above the music.

'Any time,' said Robert, taking a notebook out of his pocket. 'Three euros,' he wrote in the careful hand of a pre-computer bookkeeper. 'Owed to Englishman.' Somehow I doubted that we were going to squeeze a Schloss-saving amount out of reckless Robert.

Chapter 4

Blonde Girls in Saunas

I liked the way Lena looked when she was on the building site: straight out of a Socialist Realism poster, the kind that has a very enthusiastic rosy-cheeked female worker advertising the Five Year Plan. Her hair hidden under a scarf. A red lumberjack shirt, heavy-duty jeans held up by braces and turned up at the bottoms; Doc Martens; a drill in her hand. For a fleeting moment I felt guilty about abandoning her to go to Berlin.

Only for a few seconds though. After coming back to Doris's apartment the previous night, I had forensically examined my body in the bathroom. Grime and chalk under my nails. Scratch marks over my chest and back from carrying sacks and ripping out pipes that had a tendency to spring back and attack you like rattlesnakes. I looked like a Renaissance picture of Saint Sebastian punctured by arrow wounds, beaten by clubs. I was perhaps a few kilos heavier than poor old Sebastian, but the resemblance was striking. So I was pleased to have an excuse to drive to Berlin and recover from my wounds; manual work was not really my talent.

'Lutz will look after you,' I said, 'won't you, Lutz?' With his lopsided walk and his crafty smile, I had become fond of the old seaman. He had a readiness to tackle new problems, which I thought of as somehow untypically Ossi. In fact, after only a few weeks, I had come to see that successful Ossis were constantly re-inventing themselves. They had no choice: no other European people had so much redundant knowledge. As a sailor in the old days he had an encyclopaedic grasp of the black market rates for Russian roubles, golden dental fillings and Bulgarian leva; he knew how to sell at a profit DDR Goldfuchs jeans on the Moscow–Odessa train and use the cash to buy crates of leather jackets in Istanbul. Now it was all just useless information. After the Wende, he sold smuggled cigarettes in East Berlin, installed satellite dishes, took out windows and put in double glazing. Now everybody could watch trash TV in rooms free of draughts. Nobody needed Lutz anymore, except for me. I was desperate for Lutz, or at least someone who understood electricity and who could saw through a plank without drawing blood or losing a thumb. And Lutz was desperate for me; for cash of course, but also for some kind of standing in Alt-Globnitz. We seemed to trust each other.

He gave a mock flat-palmed maritime salute.

'Aye, aye, captain.'

'I'll be back tomorrow,' I told Lena, not able to read her face, but imagining her to be unhappy, 'this is not a trip up the Amazon, just up the Spree.'

'Just go,' said Lena, waving a hand impatiently, 'but make sure you come back with our very own Five Year Plan.'

Because that was the point of my mission: to come up with a way of making the Schloss an attractive destination and a profitable business. We weren't going to be able to persuade the Alt-Globnitz Sparkasse to part with any cash before we could present some serious figures. Lena and I both sensed it could work; the place felt right. God knows that it was rare enough that Lena and I were on the same wavelength. We were a classic case of opposites in magnetic attraction. She hated sitting close to the cinema screen. I favoured the third row. She forgot faces and confused names; I have a pathological memory for warts, hanging eyelids, the shape of noses, and hope one day to put my skills at the disposal of Scotland Yard. Me: bored in museums. She: drifts in a trance from room to room in the Neue Galerie. She loves spinach and broccoli; I think the colour green should be banished from dinner plates. Before I can drive a car, I go through good-luck rituals and in vivid stomach-curdling detail, rehearse the kind of problems that might await me on the route. Lena by contrast drives barefooted in the summer, a free spirit on the Landstrasse. It was thus a kind of a miracle that we were both now convinced of the merits of the Schloss, despite its apparently hopeless condition. The challenge was to persuade others that we weren't crazy. Hence the brainstorming session in Berlin, not just with Harry – brainstorming with him usually ended with that most sensitive of human organs being shut down by a couple of bottles of Chateau Amnesia – but also with an old university friend, Simon MacGregor. As I drove through the woodland of Brandenburg, Carla Bruni crooning on the Opel's tape deck, I thought back to the last time that I saw my university contemporary, a freckled pompous Highlander. It had been almost exactly two years earlier, at a New Year's Party in Edinburgh. Mutual friends: a couple of doctors with a drink problem, though they preferred to diagnose it as an erratic surge of adrenaline. Whatever the cause, they ended up reliving their wild student days on 31 December every year, climbing up clock towers in their underpants or shouting obscenities from a rooftop.

The Scots take Hogmanay more seriously than the English, treating it as an occasion to enter oblivion for the first three days of the year. Those blacked-out days are the perfect time for a foreign country to declare war on Scotland; the country is comatose, the porridge untouched, the bagpipes silent. Since I couldn't understand what most Scotsmen were saying, even when they were sober, I sat in a corner and started to send a text message to Lena. We had only just met, but already I felt a need to communicate with her. Then I spotted Simon, the only vertical Scot in the room, earnestly introducing himself to a young equally freckled woman. He was explaining his job to the woman – with such passion that, against all the odds, she seemed interested in Simon. The gist of his chat-up patter was this: he was an expert in the modern craft of nation-branding, a PR man who packaged countries rather than washing powder. 'Just came back from Iran,' he was saying. 'My God, it's difficult to give the mullahs sex appeal.' The woman was duly fascinated. I wanted to tell her: don't mate with this man! Your child will be one giant freckle! Instead I just politely edged into their conversation. She gave me a keep-away stare. Simon, apparently pleased to see me, said he was moving to Germany, and we vowed to meet up, exchanged business cards. In the event, we never did link up in Berlin; we both travelled too much. But after my session at Gundi's, I had suddenly remembered him. Of course! If anyone could sell Brandenburg, it was Simon. A man who could make the beardies of Tehran seem like fun-loving partygoers, Simon should be on our side. I phoned him up.

'It's an emergency,' I told him. And, suddenly, it was.

The three of us, Harry, Simon and myself, had arranged to meet for a drink at Lutter and Wegner, which looks out onto the Gendarmenmarkt. This was where the lawyer-writer E. T. A. Hoffmann had his Berlin hang-out after finishing work at the inns of court. Harry was impressed when I told him that the multi-talented Hoffmann used to order alcohol according to what he was writing at the table: old Rheinwein if he was composing church music, champagne if he was writing comic sketches, southern wines if he was writing Lieder, Burgundy for operas.

In the days when Hoffmann ruled the roost, the ideas and wine flowed until six in the morning. In our days, the days of modern global crisis, the hours were more carefully rationed and the talk cramped by the presence of insolvency attorneys and 'restructuring specialists' hoping to pick some meat from between the spare ribs of Germany's sickly car industry.

So there was some surprise at the neighbouring tables when two bottles of Burgundy appeared on our table. Liquid lunches languidly enjoyed: that seemed like a flashback to a different era; 2006, perhaps, when people had time and money. Since Harry was in paid employment he had offered to foot the bill ('I'll put it on expenses and pretend I was entertaining Angela Merkel's dentist').

'Burgundy it is, then!' said Harry summoning the waiter, and telling him to bring us lamb chops as well as the wine.

'Your Ossi ruin will end up as grand opera, you mark my words!'

'As long as it doesn't end up as Macbeth's castle with corpses lying around.'

'Ah, here comes Macbeth himself,' said Harry, spotting Simon floating slowly through the restaurant, pausing only to give unwanted advice to the wine waiter.

'MacGregor,' I said, 'try to remember that. Be nice to him. He could be important to this project.'

'What Schloss is this?' boomed Simon, when he joined us, having evidently picked up a bit of our conversation. 'We Scots love castles.'

With a slight wheeze, Simon drew up a chair and I explained the situation to him. Brandenburg, he admitted, was a tough nut to crack, perhaps tougher than the mullahs.

Simon wanted us to pay attention. If a good wine was what it took to keep us alert, then so be it. But he wanted us to sit up straight, stiff-backed like himself.

'Let's take Finland,' he said, reviewing his portfolio of difficult states, 'What's the first thing that comes to your mind?'

'Vodka,' said Harry.

'Blonde girls in saunas,' I said.

'Blonde girls drinking vodka in the sauna and gabbling an incomprehensible language into their Nokias,' said Harry.

'While listening to Sibelius,' I chipped in.

'Sib who?' asked Harry.

'You see,' said Simon, 'you've already reached the limit of nice things to say about Finns. If you add high rates of depression, alcoholism and suicide and throw in a few school massacres – that after all is how Finland comes over in the international media – then you have an image problem. So what do you do?'

'Get more pretty Finnish girls into the newspapers,' said Harry who was fast losing interest in the conversation. He could not stand Simon's professorial style of conversation ('We're not in a bloody TV quiz show,' he whispered to me, 'why doesn't he just make his point?'). But I needed Simon's advice. Because the essential problem was how to get the British to come to Brandenburg when even Germans shunned the place.

'No,' said Simon. Harry groaned and I glared at him. 'You present an alternative Finn, lighter, self-mocking. What do they do now, thanks to the advice of nation-branders?'

'Tell us,' said Harry, 'just tell us.'

'They have world sauna championships. They have Nokia-throwing competitions. There is even an international wife-carrying contest. Helsinki is seen as the European capital of Irony. Add that to funny, sexy acts in the Eurovision Song Contest and you get a situation where every third member of the European Union would like to meet a Finn.'

'Yeah. Once,' grunted Harry. 'And preferably not in a classroom.'

'Somehow I can't see wife-carrying races catching on in eastern Germany,' I said.

'They'd have to queue up for the women,' said Harry. 'And they'd have to lose a bit of weight.'

'Well, don't take me too literally,' said Simon, making a show of sniffling his wine. 'What is your aim? To convert the popular image of Ossis as a tribe...'

'A collection of tribes,' I interrupted, 'don't oversimplify.'

'A collection of tribes connected by a morose world-view, a suspicion of foreigners and a morbid resentment of anything new, into a vibrant region with a long history, that is – I'm sorry to keep using this word – sexy and open to change. How do we do that? We turned the Finns from murdering depressives into depressives with a sense of humour, right?'

'Some of the world's best comedians were depressives,' said Harry, showing interest in the conversation for the first time.

'Exactly!' said Simon, and Harry glowed with pleasure, like a schoolboy who had been praised for his grasp of calculus. 'If we show the Ossis that it is not only normal to be depressive but also, just possibly, a sign of genius, then we have won half the battle. So what we do is introduce them to other cultures with low self-esteem...'

'The British,' I said.

'The Scots,' said Harry, looking pointedly at Simon MacGregor.

'... and let them discover their commonalities. The result will be some kind of almost erotic tension. And Brandenburg, poor arid Brandenburg, will look the place to be. See it as an inter-cultural experiment,' said Simon, causing Harry to splutter some of his fine inky forty-euros-a-bottle wine onto the crisp linen tablecloth. 'You are going to have to be very sensitive, very selective. The B and B has to be seen as a benign colonial outpost, the beginning of a cultural revolution.'

Even at university, Simon had been incapable of any normal student activity – beer, wine, poker, picking up au pair girls, sleeping late – without attaching a theoretical framework. He even used the German word: *Überbau*. He had an extraordinary talent for irritating men, and for impressing women. Not just the almost always available women from the Young Conservatives association (who were determined to expand their sexual experience before settling down with a young, chinless aristocrat) but also the far more difficult members of the Marxist-Leninist Society. It was this special insight into the minds and hidden desires of the crazy Left that had steered me towards Simon. He was going to be my Brandenburg-guru.

'OK,' he said slowly as if I were particularly backward. 'I shall spell this out for you in very simple terms. So simple' – he glared over to Harry – 'that I will accept no interruptions.'

We nodded glumly. Harry twitched his head towards a waiter indicating that there was a pressing need for more Burgundy.

'The East Germans were bullied around by landowners, then by the Nazis, colonised by the Soviet Union and then by the West Germans who wanted to privatise everything lock, stock and barrel. So all their training tells them: we hate colonialism. But you know, and I know, and they know that colonialism is not all bad. It gets schools built, and decent roads, and – how shall I say this – sets up a pattern of responsibility between the exploiter and the supposedly exploited. Do you follow so far?'

Harry was looking out of the window at the Gendarmenmarkt. A group of well-fed Americans was rambling across the square, panting after only a few paces. Harry pinioned the remains of his lamb chop to a fork and waved it, causing some of the tourists to turn towards us enviously. If they had been dogs their tongues would have lolled out. As it was, their jaws merely slipped open in the usual transatlantic manner.

'Yes, yes,' I said to Simon. 'Go on.'

'So if you go to an East German country town now, your Alt-Globnitz for example, and say: look, we can transform your lives, in the British Empire we had three centuries of experience in building up failed states and uniting tribes, they're going to say: Fuck off, you're British and we're not going to sell our souls to imperialists. Right?'

'I suppose so.' My attention was on Harry who was now making a performance of eating his meat very slowly and with mimed enjoyment while the hungry Yanks clustered around the window, ignoring their guide.

Simon steamed on regardless. He was in full flow.

'But actually the Ossis want you there. British interest makes them feel wanted. Plus: East Germans don't like West Germans and the British don't like West Germans, right? Fits together, no? So here's the plan. First you have to show that Britain and Brandenburg are kindred spirits. Did you know that the writer Theodor Fontane was a correspondent in London?'

I didn't.

'Yes, well, literature was always your weak spot at Uni.'

'Thanks, Simon.' I exchanged glances with Harry. ('Punch him on the nose,' he whispered to me.)

Simon failed to spot that he had briefly lost the attention of his audience.

'Apparently Fontane was a great admirer of *The Times*, used to copy bits of it. Then he went on to be a war correspondent. Franco-Prussian war. I'm surprised you didn't know this.'

'How does this help?'

'Simple: he's an Anglo-German hero! He belongs to Brandenburg and he belongs to the British too. And you know what that means? Money!'

Harry brightened.

'So here's what you do. You get a brass plaque made, announcing that your Schloss is now the seat of the Brandenburg British-German Friendship Society and you nail it to the gate. You spread rumours that Fontane once stayed in the Schloss on his famous wanderings. It doesn't matter if it's true or not. You get a website and an email address – and you get working on special events. A Fontane Fish-and-Chips evening, a British car rally around *Effi Briest* territory. And of course you hang the Union Jack from the front of the house.' Simon paused, examined our blank faces. '*Effi Briest*, being Fontane's masterpiece. A love story. Germany's Madame Bovary. Or Anna Karenina. Adultery Lit.'

I dimly remembered the story of Effi – a joyful teenager who marries a dry stick of an aristocrat twenty years older than her. After years of being lectured by her Baron, she has an affair with a womanising cavalry officer, Major Crampas. The fling is eventually discovered, the Baron divorces her, she is shunned, falls ill, dies. The Baron kills Crampas in a duel. Just about everybody ends up unhappy.

Brilliant, I thought, we could offer feel-good weekends for the British.

'You'd have to be pretty depressive to be obsessed with Effi Briest,' I said.

'Nonsense,' said Simon. 'The English love women like her; it's the Princess Diana complex. Beautiful young woman, wild, natural, childish, trapped in a marriage with a well-born bore, dies tragically. Pulls all the heart strings.'

I was still a little doubtful.

'Most of the English have never heard of Fontane,' I said doubtfully. They probably think he's a football player.

Harry nodded.

'Goalkeeper for Potsdam United.'

'Doesn't matter,' said Simon. 'If you have established a literary connection, you get subsidies and grants: from the British Council, from the Goethe Institute, who knows, maybe

UNESCO will pay for your roof. And since you are advancing the cause of British culture in East Germany...'

'A developing country,' chipped in Harry.

'... you can expect some kind of British government help as well. The British consul is an old friend. I'll see if I can get him to come to the Schloss. He's a Highlander like me, always wears a kilt. It'll drive those East German women wild. Always works when I wear it.'

'What do you think, Harry?' He was trying to wrestle a bit of lamb from between his front teeth and took his time answering me.

'Sounds good to me,' he said at last, 'I'm all for screwing cash out of the British government.'

'That's the spirit!' exclaimed Simon. 'Think of yourself as a coloniser. They've had the Russians – now for the British! And you know what? We'll do it better! I'll come down myself to lend a hand.'

'Right,' I said, 'let's drink to that.'

Harry made a grab for the Burgundy.

'To Fontane Towers!' I said.

'To Fonty Towers and fish and chips for the hungry natives!' said Harry.

'Glad to be of help,' said Simon.

Chapter 5

The Mayor and the Frogs

In Alt-Globnitz we were, it seemed, no longer part of a freak show to be avoided by all sensible citizens. Instead, we had graduated to the status of crazy foreigners willing to spend money in the town. This was promotion. I had half-expected a peasants' revolt with the locals driving us out of town with pitchforks. But there had been cautious attempts to study the odd Engländer. Horst had taken to coming round to the building site for chats about the drumming techniques of Charlie Watts. He was beginning to exhaust my knowledge of Rolling Stones trivia and get on the nerves of Lena. But he was always happy to run an errand. The same went for Peter the Plumber – who was supposed to be sorting out the blocked showers – and Reckless Robert the bank manager. Although technically employed, they seemed to have endless amounts of time for a lunchtime or early evening beer. Not that this generated Oscar Wildean levels of conversation. Sometimes we could sit for half an hour – I would disappear to the lavatory to check my BlackBerry – exchanging barely twenty words about the political decline of Germany. But it was a bonding of sorts, an end to our Splendid Isolation. The curiosity in Alt-Globnitz had burst through the natural reserve of the locals. Normally the Ossi was too proud to ask questions of strangers. To do so was a loss of face, an admission that one didn't know everything. Now there was a noticeable thaw.

Was Prince Harry coming to stay in the new British Schloss? The cashier in the supermarket, a pasty-faced twenty-year-old, wanted to know. The queue at the cash desk pretended not to care, but their ears twitched.

'Perhaps,' I said, not yet ready to disappoint my audience. 'Perhaps not, he has a complicated love life.'

The cashier, who had a small bulging stomach that hinted of her own complicated love life, nodded sympathetically. She scanned my beans.

'So there will be reporters from *Bunte*?' This was Germany's glossy celebrity weekly.

'And *Hello*,' I said, apologetically. 'It will soon be St Moritz in the winter, St Tropez in the summer, Alt-Globnitz in the autumn.'

'Why only then?' asked a bony, sharp-nosed woman in the queue.

I wanted to say: 'Look around – do you see the ski slopes? The sandy beaches? When was the last time anyone wore sunglasses in Alt-Globnitz?'

Instead I said: 'Autumn is the most beautiful season in the Brandenburg.'

'He's right', said someone in the queue.

Next time Lena could do the shopping.

The vital information gleaned in the queue trickled through the village gossip exchange; some said a party should be organised for the royal visitor; the left-wingers, meanwhile, said that Alt-Globnitz should shun Prince Harry just as soon as he arrived and a 'Hands off Afghanistan' placard should be strung from the Rathaus. Only the mayor did not have a view. He was strangely absent from our lives. Why wasn't he more enthusiastic about the re-invention of his town?

Decisive for the change of village mood was our shift from the 'holiday apartment' of Doris Bonkerz to the Schloss. The Schloss was not ready but it was increasingly absurd to live with Doris just to spare ourselves some discomfort. For one thing, Doris – university-educated, sharp-tongued – was viewed with some trepidation by the village. Lena and I were outsiders living with a semi-outsider. If we wanted the respect of Alt-Globnitz we had to become masters of our domain. It would certainly speed up the work.

And so we were sleeping in the Schloss. Our bedroom was ready, but it wasn't yet able to provide a good night's rest.

The countryside is noisy at night; it was like living in a disco full of screeching teenagers. Owls shrieking out an avian version of to-be-or-not-to-be: *Hamlet* on speed. Cats, perhaps Stasi-trained, jumping on and executing their rodent victims. Foxes searching dustbins for non-recycled food. Mac appeared to be the only sleeping animal on our terrain and even he was making a racket, breathing in deeply and then emitting a long, shuddering snore. Lena had placed his basket in our bedroom, saying he would feel more secure. Maybe it was Lena herself who needed the sensation of inhabiting a warm nest, all the brood gathered together.

The house had become our baby but the baby was still a stranger. As darkness fell, the questions started to eat away at us: was the house, the new life, too much for us? Not everybody was capable of re-inventing him- or herself. It could be that I was doomed to be an urban neurotic, drawn compulsively to petrol fumes, to the smell of urine in multi-storey car parks, to flickering neon. All I knew was: I could sleep in the city, but not in the country. It was two o'clock in the morning and my limbs were still as hard as wooden splints, my brain on standby, and outside the nocturnal animal world was squealing and howling. I gently levered my way out of bed, threaded my way past Mac, grabbed a jumper and went on to the balcony. The air was clean, you could sense that, but not odourless. Foxes smelled, so did cats. Why didn't cats hibernate over winter? Suddenly a rustling in the bushes disturbed my random sleep-deficient thought pattern. Twigs were breaking near the side of the pond and there was a kind of grunting, a snorting. A wild boar? But wasn't it too early in the year for them? And hadn't they all moved to the suburbs of Berlin, to run wild in the garden allotments and barge their way into restaurant kitchens? I peered into the gloom, wishing I had put on my glasses. Slowly, very slowly, a shape emerged; on two legs, but smaller than a bear – and cursing quietly in German. A burglar? No! Lutz! He seemed to reach downwards, pick up something from a patch of muddy soil, put it in his pocket. What was Lutz doing in my garden in the early hours of the morning? Calling out to him didn't seem like an option. It would disturb the natural nocturnal ecology, wake up Lena and perhaps tell me something about Lutz that I didn't want to know. So I watched him for a while. He seemed to be making a clucking noise, to be looking at the ground. Once he looked up to stare at the half-moon, sliced as precisely as pizza. Minute by minute I was growing colder, a chill attacking my pyjama trousers, and less curious about Lutz's antics. Slipping behind the glass door without attracting Lutz's attention, I tried to rub myself warm and went down the rotting staircase to make myself a toasted ham and cheese sandwich. The toast burned. That night I dreamed that Lutz was a werewolf, hunting my soul.

The next morning, the world looked a little less menacing. That too was part of country living: nights were often mysterious, days were often boring. Lena told me that I had been talking in my sleep. 'What sleep?' I asked. While we drank coffee she gave me my orders. It was to be my task over the coming days to furnish the upstairs bedrooms. Tastefully. Simply. It seemed to be a bit early, since the top floor still hadn't been renovated. Why strain the credit cards now? But Lena was adamant. If we were to be a credible B and B, she said, we had to have a place to fry breakfast and beds to sleep on. I couldn't argue with this logic but dreaded the prospect of entering the blue-and-yellow hell-gates of IKEA.

'Right,' I told Lena whose eyes were shifting colour from grey to green, an extraordinary trick which usually signified that she was thinking about curtains and bay poles. 'I'm going to survey the garden first though. You carry on brooding about curtains.'

'How – how did you know?' Lena was genuinely astonished. I had never told her about my ability to read her eyes. In fact I don't think she even realised that they changed colour, and I certainly wasn't planning to tell her. Sometimes men have to stay ahead of the curve, unsettle women with secret reservoirs of knowledge.

I shrugged, gave a tight secret smile and walked towards the pond with Mac sniffing at my heels.

Lutz was standing, looking at the greenish placid water, absolutely still like an Apache scout listening for the distant rumble of buffalo.

'You look tired, Lutz,' I said. Actually he seemed perfectly normal – jeans, fleece, unshaven, skin a little grey; Lutz's usual Tuesday morning image. 'Bad night?'

'No, I slept fine,' he said.

'Aha.'

There was a pause while I tried to work out whether this was a lie or not.

'But there's something on your mind?'

Lutz shook his head. It was his turn to look at me quizzically.

'You have been given some unpleasant task by Miss Lena?'

'Yes,' I said grimly and pretended to make the sign of the cross. 'IKEA.' It was just a lame reflex joke to show my abhorrence of the Swedish flat-pack torture-shop but a thought flashed through my mind, the shard of a dream: what if Lutz was a werewolf? What if he knew that I knew he was a werewolf? Absurd.

'Sorry,' I said, meaning: sorry for making a religious gesture in jest.

'It's OK,' said Lutz, though he didn't smile. 'You're looking for a reason, I think, not to go to the shop.'

'Spot on!' I said.

'I hate the place too. It makes me feel like a prisoner.'

Werewolf or no werewolf, Lutz and I were kindred spirits.

'I was in the garden last night,' said Lutz.

'Really?' I said.

'Found this.' Out of his pocket he pulled out a plastic bag. Inside was a dead frog.

'Female,' he said. I noticed it was big, maybe ten centimetres. He flipped the bag over and showed me the slightly yellow stomach that signified a female. 'The frogs are growing faster than I've ever seen them before. So I was curious. You can only understand frogs when you watch them at night – but you know that.'

I did. Frogs had a great nightlife.

'And I saw the first frogs mating. It's only February and the mating season is already starting.'

'It must be the global warming thing.'

Lutz nodded. He knew that the weather was going crazy. Rain rather than snow now in the winter, followed by bone dry Aprils and Mays and, since the sandy earth couldn't store water, drought in the summer. The past year had been so bad that there wasn't enough hay to feed the horses. Doris Bonkerz had complained to Lena and me that she couldn't go riding anymore: the stables which a few years ago were seen as being a potential magnet for teenage tourists had been shut down. Fodder had become too expensive.

Now it seemed that the wildlife was going haywire.

'You understand what it means if the mating season is going to start early?' asked Lutz.

'The big migration.' Following their instincts, programmed to return to the same lake or pond to mate and lay eggs, frogs zigzag their way from their winter resting places. It is an astonishing sight, a bit like watching Germans head for the Autobahn on the first day of school holidays. But our frogs would have to cross the road to reach the Schloss, spelling certain death given the legendary driving skills of the Brandenburgers. It was difficult enough for humans.

'They think it's spring, the stupid buggers,' said Lutz. 'Who knows when they'll start to march – maybe the next big rain.'

'And then – SPLAT!'

Lutz nodded grimly.

'We could set up buckets along the roadside. Then when they come, I'll stop the traffic and you scoop them up with a fishing net and drop them into the buckets and Lena can take them to the pond.'

'Wouldn't work here,' said Lutz. 'You'd get run down too. Anyway who knows when it will happen? We can't just stop work every time there's a possible frog alert.'

We thought about this silently for a while. I walked with Lutz to an ornamental stone bench that Lena had ordered for the terrace. I flinched as I sat on the coldness of the stone and watched Lutz methodically roll a cigarette, spitting on the paper to make it stick.

'You want one?' he asked, after spitting again, this time on the floor.

'Er, no thanks.' I could have used a cigarette. But not one smothered in Lutz's DNA. 'You know what I think...'

'Yes,' said Lutz, before I could finish the sentence. 'You think you should go to the mayor and get a sign put up warning drivers to go slowly because of invading frogs.'

'How did you know?'

'Because even a visit to the scumbag mayor is better than going to IKEA.'

I had heard some odd reports about the mayor. The hairdresser had told Lena that he had a reputation as a ladies' man. In Brandenburg that meant any man who had eight euros to spare for a bunch of drooping tulips from the petrol station. The only woman who admitted to having been romantically connected with the mayor was Doris Bonkerz. Before leaving her Ferienwohnung to move to the Schloss, we had invited her upstairs for dinner. Lena had cooked up some *Tafelspitz*, boiled meat and vegetables served up with horseradish, and while the wind battered the imperfectly sealed windows we had pumped Doris for the inside story of Alt-Globnitz. Her father and her father's father had been pharmacists and, while the Apotheke was obviously in state ownership in DDR times, they were always regarded as pillars of society. Pharmacists knew all the tough secrets: which girls were going on the pill without their mothers' knowledge; the pregnancy tests; the haemorrhoids; the cancer scares. They were trusted more than doctors. But Doris had even more valuable knowledge. Not only had she once been Lutz's girlfriend – at about the time that Erich Honecker was making his definitive speech to the Bulgarian communist party – but the mayor had also competed for her affections. Younger, more athletic than his rival, the future mayor had been a zealous communist youth leader.

'I didn't like him,' recalled Doris, who despite her striking high cheekbones had remained resolutely unmarried from the Soviet invasion of Afghanistan, through the collapse of communism, the arrival of Aldi, the near-collapse of capitalism and the approaching breakdown of the planet's ecosystem. She had seen it all and her survival was probably linked to the fact that she had never worn a wedding ring. 'I didn't like him then and I don't like him now. He sways with the wind.'

I was beginning to understand why Lutz had such evident distaste for the mayor: they had once been rivals. More, it seemed that Lutz had been a free spirit while the future mayor had been a bit of a conformist.

'The man doesn't seem to have any edges. I sometimes wondered whether he was a kind of phantom.' Doris raised her hands as if admitting her bafflement. 'Perhaps that's what it takes to be a politician.'

He was certainly elusive. There was no doubting that he was the most powerful man in Alt-Globnitz and yet in our almost two months here I hadn't caught a glimpse of him. So it did not come as a surprise that walking through the Rathaus to his office was an almost spectral journey, past locked doors, through silent corridors. As I walked my way past the Registry of Births (soon to be merged with Deaths and Driving Licences to save money), past a room marked 'Social Matters and Miscellaneous (grass-cutting, dog littering, and garage enlargement)', then on, beyond the Women's Rights office (closed until further notice), I felt like one of the *Ghostbusters* team trying to root out a hidden supernatural enemy. The mayor's office was on the second floor, a set of three interlocking rooms. The first antechamber was occupied by a secretary. In what seemed like a single movement she took my coat, hung it up and with an economic use of words – 'Please wait here' – directed me to the second room. It was slightly darker than her room, probably lit by energy-saving bulbs, perhaps to discourage me from reading the various files that had been stacked up the walls. I tried to read them anyway and quickly realised that they were a history of crazed re-invention, a chronicle of one East German town's attempts to make itself appear attractive to the rest of the world. 'Battery-driven tricycles', said one file. 'Circus animal cemetery', said another. The most promising because it matched the Zeitgeist: 'Recovering methane gas from cows: Alt-Globnitz as a storage centre'.

'What's this one?' I asked the secretary as she broke her meditative silence to offer me tea.

Disconcertingly in a woman so young – she could barely have been a teenager when the Wall was punctured – she gave a farm-boy smirk that immediately recalled a certain former American president. I wanted to say: don't smile! Don't use your facial muscles! But I didn't, and she did.

'We invited crime writers from around Brandenburg to read at night in the graveyard at Halloween. The mayor thought it would be a good idea to market Alt-Globnitz as the scariest town east of the Elbe.'

'Did it work?' The plan did not seem bad; if you can't be the most beautiful or the smartest, why not be the most frightening?

The secretary smiled again with a downward Bushian tug. (No! Don't do it!)

'Not really. The torch battery ran out, so the novelist had to stop reading, lost his temper and banged into a stone cross. A local reporter tried to interview him, fell into an open grave and broke his leg. We ended up with three paragraphs in *Bild Zeitung*.'

'That's not bad,' I said, 'there are days when the whole of the German political world doesn't get more.'

'But they called us Alt-Horrorwitz, added ten years to the mayor's age and called him an Ossi Master of Horrors. He has been nervous about the media ever since.'

The phone rang in her office. It was the mayor ushering me into his presence. Why he couldn't have just opened the door himself and said 'Hello' remained a mystery. Nor did he rise from his chair when I entered. I could see that he had been busy on a crossword.

'I'm sorry to disturb you,' I said. The light was brighter than in the other two rooms. I remembered the trick he had of keeping his office lights on through the night to give the impression that he was constantly at his desk solving the problems of Alt-Globnitz.

'Not at all,' he said waving me to a chair and glancing at his big watch, the kind used by captains in U-boats. The room was sparely decorated – the flag of Brandenburg with its red anorexic eagle pinned to the wall, a calendar evidently given free by a garage and the crest of Alt-Globnitz, which depicted a fish, a horse and a crown. Apparently a weary duke had been hunting in the region; his horse had become lame, and the Kurfürst had had to spend the night. He was fed a trout that had been caught in the Oder and choked on a bone. A hefty Alt-Globnitz housewife was the only person who dared to hit the nobleman and, in banging him hard in the back, had ejected the stuck trout and saved his life. Since then Alt-Globnitz had been allowed to call itself a town but it was banned, by royal decree, from ever serving fish again. The rescuing housewife had been given a gold coin and soon afterwards left her husband, and the region, to find happiness elsewhere.

'A fine legend,' I told the mayor, pointing to the crest.

'It has a lesson for us,' he said. I noticed that apart from his crossword utensils, his desk was cluttered with nose sprays and vitamins and antiseptic hand-wipes. 'First, we have a tradition of re-inventing ourselves, not waiting for outsiders to come in. We have our feet on the ground, like the famous housewife. Second, problems get worse if we let our womenfolk leave to seek their fortunes in the west.'

The secretary brought in another cup of tea, unbidden. The mayor already had a glass of water, which he used to wash down a pill.

'And now,' he continued, 'you have come to Alt-Globnitz to announce that the British will save us?'

I detected a hint of cynicism in his voice.

'Actually,' I said, 'I wanted to ask you about my frogs.'

'Your frogs?'

'The frogs. They will be soon migrating across the main road into the Schloss.'

The mayor did not seem very interested in the frogs.

'Perhaps you should first explain to me what you are doing with your Schloss. I understand that you are turning it into a Gasthaus.'

'Not exactly – a bed and breakfast.'

The mayor looked blank. He reached underneath the crossword and took out a sheaf of papers.

'Let me tell you exactly what you are required to do if you intend to turn the Schloss into a Gasthaus…'

'A B and B.'

'Police licensing approval.'

'A what?'

'That is compulsory if you are going to serve alcohol.'

The mayor started to recite the many, many pieces of paper that we were going to have to find.

'A statement from the Inland Revenue that your taxes were in order is absolutely essential,' he said.

'In order?' I thought of Harry and the many adventures we had gone through in the past in order to meet the German definition of being orderly.

'I will need to see your ground plans,' continued the mayor. 'I will need to be satisfied that you are not destroying a historic building.'

'In fact our plan is to stop a historic building falling down.'

'There are plans and there are plans,' said the mayor cryptically.

'I will need a Commercial Usage Registration Form of course.'

'Of course.'

'Your staff...'

'What staff?'

'Your staff will have to take a hygiene course. Directive 43 Paragraph 1 of the infections and diseases protection law,' said the mayor, reading from his list. It seemed to be as long as an Icelandic saga. 'Anyone working in the kitchen, or even touching food, has, of course, to get an approval certificate from Health and Hygiene.'

'The bed and breakfast concept,' I explained, 'it's more of a family thing. People come to stay. Relax.'

The mayor grimaced.

'These rules are made for a reason: it is my responsibility as mayor to ensure that strangers do not bring chaos or diseases into the country.' He started to read from the documents, more to himself than to me, morbidly fascinated by the infection laws: 'Stool samples... salmonella... shingles... E. coli bacteria... cholera.'

'Ebola fever,' I added for good measure. 'Anthrax.'

'Typhus,' continued the mayor relentlessly, 'Hepatitis A.'

He interrupted to take out an antiseptic wipe and cleaned his hands.

'Dangerous places, kitchens,' I said.

'Very,' said the mayor, taking my comment seriously.

'You can never be too careful,' he continued. 'If you have an eating or drinking space of fifty square metres you will have to construct at least one toilet for handicapped people. That is...' he studied the small print, '... it must be at least eight square metres.' And then there is the staff toilet. No dogs in the kitchen area...' The mayor paused and raised his glasses. He was obviously aware of Mac and his tendency to hunt for food in the house.

'Shall I continue?'

'No thanks,' I said. 'I think you will find that I have a constitutional right to invite people onto my property and to feed them.'

'But if you seek to profit from this enterprise, you have to obey the law,' said the mayor. 'And I must tell you that much of the control institutions are based in this Rathaus. My Rathaus.'

Suddenly, the mayor had put his cards on the table. He was letting us know that he could easily destroy our Schloss project. It could take months to collect all the various pieces of paper from his officials. What was he after? A bribe?

'Look,' I said, 'all we want to do is bring some life to Alt-Globnitz. Attract some international interest. Bring money to the place.'

'You think there is no life here?' I thought of the cemetery next to the Schloss. The way it was divided between the graves of those who had relatives in the west – finely tended plants, regularly watered over the years in return for care packages from the west – and the neglected mossy stones and crosses of those without families abroad. I thought about the town's shrinking Kindergarten and the fact that Doris Bonkerz's biggest-selling items were orthopaedic shoes, false teeth cleaning liquid and Zimmer frames.

'Well you have pond life,' I said. 'You have great pond life.'

The mayor stood up for the first time. He was quite short with what seemed to be skinny legs; his torso though was muscular, the veins bulging out of his neck like a slab of good uncooked steak. If ever I got into a fight with him, I thought, I would have to kick his knees and then make a run for it before he got to use his strangler's hands. Not my usual thinking process, but there was some coiled aggression about him, a testosterone surplus. Perhaps I was misjudging him. Perhaps he was trying to think of a Siberian river with four letters.

'I have a proposal,' he said. 'You have to finish your roof, correct?'

I nodded.

'You need a team of workers for a month. Don't get them from Poland, get them from Alt-Globnitz. There are enough youths here without work. It will cost you more but it will show you want to contribute to the local community.'

He shuffled around on his desk again and wrote a name and number on a scrap of paper.

'That's Uwe, he can be your foreman.'

'I think it's up to me who I put in charge.' Thinking: Lutz will go crazy if I install someone else. The idea of accelerating the Schloss repairs with a sudden surge of workers was not a bad one, though.

'You can trust Uwe. He's my brother-in-law.'

At last I began to understand the thrust of the conversation. If I helped him out, he would not throw the rule book at me.

'Well, in that case, I look forward to meeting Uwe and his merry men,' I said, displaying more good cheer than I felt. 'And the frogs?'

'Take care of some of Alt-Globnitz's human inhabitants and we can talk about the lives of its frogs.'

'Right!' I said. 'That sounds like a deal to me!' I reached forward to shake his hand but he drew back abruptly as if I had offered garlic to a closet vampire. My hand stayed hovering in space for a few uncomfortable seconds and I realised my time was up. As I left I glimpsed the mayor wiping his hands again, killing the germs.

Chapter 6

Our Man in Berlin

There was good news and there was bad news. The good news was that I had won my duel-by-correspondence with the British Ambassador in Berlin. It had begun innocently enough. The Schloss, I had told him, was a unique cultural experiment in Brandenburg: we were trying to extend the outer borders of the civilised world, bringing Britain to the heathens. Surely that was worth a few euros?

'Thank you so much for your letter,' came the succinct reply. 'We wish you all the best with your project.' Signed by the Secretary to the Ambassador. I did not give up.

* * * * *

Schloss Alt-Globnitz

Dear Ambassador,

Without seeming forward, I had hoped for a more enthusiastic approach. We are planning no less than the complete transformation of an admittedly small part of Brandenburg into a showcase for Britain. We hope to raise public awareness that Theodor Fontane learned his craft in England. No Englishman has set foot in this place since Queen Victoria sent one of her emissaries to search for suitable Prussian mates for her children. We are doing pioneer work and we need your financial support...

* * * * *

His Excellency the British Ambassador, Berlin

Dear Sir,

Thank you for your note. Britain has always taken a keen interest in Queen Victoria who as you probably know had a railway station named after her in London. Our problem is that you seem to be providing accommodation for English football fans – we assume that this Fontane character is one of their violent models? – and naturally cannot be involved in such a project...

* * * * *

Schloss Alt-Globnitz

Dear Ambassador,

Thank you for your kind words. Of course we do understand that Britain doesn't have much cash at the moment. And no, we are not setting up a hotel for British football fans. If anything we hope to introduce sports like croquet and Highland Dancing to the region.

P. S. Fontane was a German writer. You might like to get your secretary to google him.

* * * * *

His Excellency the British Ambassador, Berlin

Dear Sir,

Thank you for your letter. We will certainly keep an eye out for this Fontane chap. Please accept an interesting new book, *Queen Victoria and the English Garden*, which we hope will bring you inspiration...

* * * * *

Schloss Alt-Globnitz

Dear Ambassador,

Thank you for the book, which might one day prove useful or even readable. I would urge you again to consider sponsoring this project in Brandenburg, which we believe could transform British public diplomacy in the region...

* * * * *

His Excellency the British Ambassador, Berlin

Dear Sir,

Thank you for your letter. The ambassador regrets that he is unable to answer it personally since he will be travelling in West Germany for the next few months and will have no time to read correspondence...

Signed Ms B Philpot, Secretary to the Ambassador

'Simon,' I said on the phone, 'what can I do? The man is as thick as an elephant's rump. Where does the Foreign Office get these people? From some farm specialising in inbred bureaucrats?'

'Actually,' said Simon, 'he is my wife's cousin.'

'Ah,' I said. 'Well, he does have very pretty notepaper.'

There was a short silence. Simon, I guessed, was thinking about my next move.

'Look,' he said at last, 'why don't you email the Prime Minister. I was at school with him. It could help.'

Schloss Alt-Globnitz

Dear Prime Minister,

I am writing to you as a great admirer of the Cameron clan. Ever since the Camerons fought the Hanoverians at the Battle of Prestonpans in 1745, I have been a fan. It took the Camerons to stand up to Hanover (such a boring place)! Simon MacGregor recommended that I approach you. No doubt you will be aware that the French are trying to spread their influence in eastern Germany to realise Charles de Gaulle's vision of building a French-run Europe from the Atlantic to the Urals. Under the previous government we abandoned our historic struggle with foreigners and now the results are unfortunately clearly visible: baguettes and croissants are on sale everywhere in East Germany. Germans drive more Renaults and Peugeots than Range Rovers. I do think it is time to show the flag.

I am doing my own bit by building a cultural embassy in Brandenburg, under the guise of a bed and breakfast. This is only the beginning! I have every hope that this could make Britain a significant player in Europe again. Sadly the ambassador in Berlin has failed to grasp the major geopolitical dimension of our project. Can I count on your support?

* * * * *

10, Downing Street, London, W1

The Prime Minister has asked me to pass on his thanks for your email. We do indeed believe there is important work to be done in eastern Germany. The Prime Minister will pass on his concern about the growing French influence in Brandenburg to the Foreign Secretary...

Signed Peter Blotto, Special Adviser

* * * * *

Schloss Alt-Globnitz

Dear Mr Blotto,

Thank you for your encouragement. I fear that the British Ambassador may not understand the urgency of our project. Some East German farmers have started to supply tonnes of snails to restaurants in France, intensifying cooperation between Paris and Brandenburg. There is really no time to lose.

* * * * *

His Excellency the British Ambassador, Berlin

Dear Sir,

I understand you need assistance for a British-Brandenburg cultural project. It is a great pity that you had not mentioned this before since our budget year is now reaching a close. We nonetheless have an open ear for anything that improves Britain's standing in the east...

* * * * *

Schloss Alt-Globnitz

Dear Ambassador,

Thank you so much for your sudden interest in my British-Ossi cultural centre. I will be sure to mention it to the Prime Minister when I communicate with him later this week.

* * * * *

His Excellency the British Ambassador, Berlin

Dear Sir,

The ambassador is pleased to inform you that some spare cash has been found in the budget for special initiatives in the east. Perhaps you could set out your most pressing priorities.

(Signed) Robert Hardup, Financial Secretary

* * * * *

Schloss Alt-Globnitz

Dear Mr Hardup,

Roof repairs 3,000 euros
Sewage 1,800 euros

Stabilisation of the first floor 800 euros
New boiler, plumbing repairs 2,300 euros
Furnishing 900 euros
Draining of frog pond 400 euros

* * * * *

British Embassy, Berlin

Dear Sir,

We have limited resources, but can offer you 2,000 euros...

(Signed) R. Hardup

* * * * *

Schloss Alt-Globnitz

Dear Mr Hardup,

I think 5,000 euros will be the sum that I will be mentioning to the Prime Minister's office in my letter this week...

* * * * *

British Embassy, Berlin

Dear Sir,

A cheque for 4,800 euros will be on its way. We will, of course, want guarantees that you are a legitimate cultural organisation. The ambassador has also asked me to send you a copy of the photo album *Great Britain: Its 50 Most Interesting Cemeteries*...

* * * * *

So that was the good news: 4,800 euros, and a book that might cure my insomnia.

The bad news: there was no longer an excuse for putting off the trip to IKEA.

Chapter 7

Swedish Meatballs

Lutz and I planned the trip to IKEA with military precision: we were leaving nothing to chance. First, obviously – obviously! – we would avoid the weekend. Early Monday morning, we concluded, was the most effective moment to trek through the deep canyons of the warehouse; that is the time of the week when most Germans can be found in doctors' waiting rooms hoping to prolong the weekend, or in banks complaining about the fact that their debit cards had been mysteriously blocked on Friday afternoon, forcing them to beg, steal or borrow cash on the weekend and eat their pet hamsters. So if there was ever a good time to find a parking space in front of IKEA, it was Monday when half the country was distracted. Second, we had a precise list of what we needed: six double beds, twelve bedside tables, twelve bedside lamps, six sets of curtains, six wardrobes. It was a big order and Lutz and I would have to make several trips in our rented van. This was going to be painful but, as with a long-delayed trip to the dentist, there was only one way to approach the task: fast and with utmost concentration. There was to be no dallying in the rubber plants, picture frames and mirror department. We had synchronised our watches: Lutz and I were determined to accomplish our mission in precisely 130 minutes; furniture commandos.

We managed to find a parking space after only two circumnavigations and – in contrast to the usual Saturday IKEA experience – without maiming anyone. In fact we were so early that we managed to grab breakfast.

'I would normally go for the köttbullars, the Swedish meatballs,' Lutz told the woman at the cash desk, 'but they give me gas. Never eat them early in the morning.'

'Thanks,' said the Kassiererin, 'I'll try to remember that.'

'Right,' I said, after ten minutes of munching a Greenland shrimp sandwich, 'let's get going.' I snatched a tape measure and a free blue-and-yellow pencil for scribbling the names of our targeted furniture.

Lutz's task was to get the beds and mattresses. I was supposed to get everything else.

'Go!'

We strode past the children's drop-off point where you can let little Björn or Astrid suffocate themselves with blue and yellow plastic balls, and into Office Equipment. Briefly pausing to see if I could move faster by sitting on a chair with wheels propelling myself forward with my feet, I noticed that Lutz was striding ahead, quietly but firmly, barging identically dressed couples to one side. We had underestimated the capacity of happily married couples in matching jumpers and, above all, pregnant women with sheepish partners to cluster on Monday mornings like zoo animals at feeding time. You could see why it happened: the shop offered them alternative birch-wood futures. As soon as you entered Home Furnishing it was impossible to escape small mock-up living rooms with sofa beds named after Swedish villages and curtains after Swedish women so that one quickly imagined oneself to be in a more cheerful version of an Ingmar Bergman movie. Without the subtitles. It all had a system, of course, and I was proud to have worked it out. Dining tables and chairs were named after Finnish places (lots of umlauts), beds and wardrobes, Lutz's responsibility, were mainly named after Norwegian towns, bathroom stuff after lakes and rivers. Jerker – a somewhat rude term in English – was a Swedish man's name and therefore, according to the IKEA code, the name of a desk.

Child's play. We rushed through Dining Rooms – frosted-glass tables, steel chairs, Billy bookcases lined with Harry Potter in Swedish – but Lutz peeled off as soon as we reached Beds. Lutz wanted to check that a bed frame called Gutvik was available.

'Gutvik?' he barked at a young woman in a flattering yellow IKEA T-shirt. 'A bed that is called Gutvik?'

'Gut... fick?' she said uncertainly. 'Here in the bed department?' *Ficken* being a crude German word for the sex act.

I left them to their verbal tangle and pushed my trolley as fast as I could to the warehouse. We were seventy minutes into Operation IKEA and, driven by some atavistic male impulse, I wanted to beat Lutz to the cash desk. There was enough oestrogen in me, however, to tempt me into throwing in a few unnecessary items – a stylish set of bathroom scales, some sharp-looking knives and, of course, scented candles – on my sprint through Bathrooms, Rugs and Flooring.

Entering the warehouse was like being an extra in a Fritz Lang movie. The vertiginous walls of flat-pack furniture seemed to move steadily closer, intent on crushing little humans, blocking out daylight. Perhaps IKEA was bound up with some chilly Lutheran saga of redemption. Upstairs you were offered the light, cheerful lifestyle. Downstairs your sinful dream was packed flat in brown recycled cardboard boxes and you were expected to suffer: to carry, to sweat, to transport and, using instructions written only in Sanskrit, to re-assemble your dream.

The priority, I decided, was to find the right -vik. There were dozens of -viks, all looking much the same in the pictures on the boxes, but Lena had been adamant that we should get Leksvik, the pseudo-antique line. Maybe she thought English guests would not be able to tell the difference. Maybe she was right.

Driving my trolley down the aisles, I imagined myself white water rafting along a canyon and was caught up in my harmless fantasy. I tried to ignore the George Orwell-inspired birdsong being piped into the warehouse. Suddenly I spotted what looked like the last of the Leksvik chest of drawers. My view was blocked a little by a meaty woman bending down trying to tug an obviously heavy stand-up mirror from the pile next to the Leksvik stuff.

'Can I help you?' I asked, for she clearly needed assistance. From behind she had seemed to be solidly built, her buttocks straining against her trousers as she huffed and puffed. Her face was sauna-pink.

'Thank you,' she panted, and with a hernia-inducing heave we transferred the mirror to her trolley. 'Careful,' she said, 'don't break anything.'

'Any time I can help,' I said, not meaning it, as I headed for the last Leksvik commode.

'Oh,' she said, 'that's mine.'

'No,' I said, 'it's lying on the shelf.'

'But I reserved it. I was just getting the mirror and then I was taking the commode.'

'This isn't the Costa del Sol,' I said, 'you can't reserve something. If I hadn't helped you with the mirror, you would still be struggling with it.'

The woman started to pull on the brown carton. As she pulled, I pushed and she lost her balance and let go. A classic martial arts technique.

'Oof,' she said, 'you pig.'

'Are you bothering my wife?'

It was a loud, deep voice. I turned round to face a man-mountain. It wasn't so much his size, bigger and broader than the biggest and broadest of IKEA wardrobes, as his obviously cruel features that bothered me. He had butcher's hands with spatulate thumbs; his lips curled and his eyes seemed to pop out of his skull. It was the face of a man who regularly lifted 20 kilograms in the fitness centre; the demeanour of a man who broke the necks of irritating kittens; the bearing of a Third World dictator. He was holding a eucalyptus plant in a white pot.

'I was actually helping your wife,' I said, but it was no good.

'Don't listen to a word, Hansi,' said his wife, 'he wanted to steal our commode.'

The man lifted me up by the lapels of my jacket and dropped me in the trolley as if I were a boy of four. Then he took a blue IKEA carrying bag, pulled it over my head and kicked the trolley so that it hurtled down the aisle and crashed into a collection of already assembled upright coat-holders and some wooden planks. There was a sickening crunch as cardboard, timber and metal pipes tumbled onto my chest.

Suddenly the IKEA birdsong fell silent.

'My God, man, what are you doing down there?' It was Lutz, and I smiled up at him like a lost alpinist greeting a St Bernard.

Lutz pulled off the furniture, tugged off the suffocating bag and looked at me, a worried crease running across his forehead.

'You don't look good,' he said, 'what the hell were you doing?'

'Leksvik,' I gasped, thinking: what if this was the last word I ever breathed? My final verbal contribution to humanity? 'I'm a victim of IKEA-rage.'

Lutz prodded my ribs. There was a slight twinge. Then he felt my pulse. I couldn't help feeling this was the wrong sequence of medical control. First, surely, see if I'm alive, then check for broken ribs.

'Can you move your neck?' This too seemed to violate the rules of First Aid. What if my neck was almost broken and I now moved it abruptly – click? Crack? But such was my trust in Lutz that I did indeed rotate my neck and nothing serious happened; nothing that is, apart from the sudden return of my short-term memory.

'Where has the monster gone?'

'He's going to complain to the manager about your sexual harassment of his wife,' said Lutz. 'Let's pay and go.'

Under the pile of wood and cardboard, the phone rang.

'I'm not interrupting anything?' asked Lena. She sounded flustered.

'No,' I croaked, 'I've got everything under control.'

'Good, because I haven't. Get back to the Schloss as soon as you can.'

Lutz and I sped back, more concerned that the kitten-killer would follow us and seek vengeance, than by the urging of Lena. Women tend to exaggerate. We all know that. Apocalypse Frau.

But in this case Lena had a point. When Lutz and I returned to the Schloss we found that all work had ground to a halt. In the days since my meeting with the mayor the renovation of the Schloss had galloped ahead. As promised, Uwe, his brother-in-law, had turned up with four young members of Horst's t'ai chi course. Uwe was older, maybe in his early thirties, a narrowed blond head, hair beginning to flee the scalp, on a pared-down body: one of those boys who go from youth to middle age without passing through manhood. He had a natural authority and the boys listened to him with an earnestness that they would not have used in conversation with their parents. Uwe had introduced the boys to me and Lena, and had immediately delegated the tasks: the staircase was to be strengthened and covered with cloth so that they could carry buckets of cement to the first floor. Two of the team – Uwe and a twenty-year-old called Toni, fresh out of the army national service – would patch up the roof and start with the insulation. And six of the upstairs bedrooms would be painted. But now Uwe was refusing to take his workers onto the roof, because there was a nest of rats in the attic. The hole in the roof had to be fixed quickly, otherwise we couldn't start to take guests.

'He can finish the roof and we'll kill the rats later,' I said.

'No, he can't,' said Lena. 'Apparently the rules are that we have to get in the Rodent Control officer; he lays traps or poison and all workers stay away for two weeks.'

'Two weeks! We can't let that happen!'

'I told you: we've got a crisis on our hands. I think we should get a humane rat trap and get rid of them ourselves.'

'Humane? What's wrong with a piece of cheese and a sharp metal trap?' Sometimes I suspected Lena of being an undercover member of Greenpeace.

'No blood. You know that I hate blood.'

'So we get a cage, put the cheese inside. Door closes when rats enter. Then what?'

'Then you take the cage and drop the rat in the pond.'

'And he humanely drowns to death. In my frog pond?' On second thoughts, there wasn't that much Greenpeace in Lena.

'Well I don't know. We must let the creatures go free somewhere. Not in Alt-Globnitz, of course.'

I could see that this job had been delegated to me; that I would be spending my afternoons cruising the Brandenburg countryside with rats in cages looking for suitably scenic exit routes. It was not exactly how I had imagined my romantic tours of Fontane Country.

'Sounds like I should have a quiet word with Uwe,' I said, and headed to the bottom of the garden. There was an old iron tub full of rainwater at one corner and the workers had made the spot into their recreation corner. The stone church wall shielded them from the wind and they had arranged some plastic garden chairs around a picnic table. On Mondays they would bring in sandwiches made by their mothers and wash them down with coffee or beer. On Wednesdays at noon they would collect cake from Lutz's wife and celebrate 'the Bergfest', literally the mountain feast, marking the exact midpoint of the working week.

They had reached the summit. Wednesday to Friday it was all downhill.

'Sorry to disturb you,' I said as I approached them. I was never quite sure what tone to adopt: the Scottish baron addressing his loyal retainers? The Czarist overseer talking to his serfs? The cotton plantation owner in Alabama? Or the friendly comprehensive schoolteacher talking to his pupils in the playground? Or as a fellow worker who just happened to be paying their wages, first among equals? I could see the workers were uneasy too. As soon as I appeared, they threw their cigarettes over the wall onto the graveyard; ashes to ashes.

'Uwe, I hear you're afraid of mice,' I said. Two of the workers sniggered. Uwe scowled.

'They were rats, roof rats,' Uwe almost hissed the words. 'Black and skinny. There's not a mouse in the world that looks like that.'

'And you think we're not capable of catching them?'

'They're nesting; soon they will be all over the place. They have to be poisoned. And as long as that's happening we can't work upstairs. That's what the rules say.' Uwe spoke confidently, as if he had memorised the law. 'You can check with the Rodent Control.'

Who, naturally, worked at the Rathaus.

'Look, I'm paying you to work. You've made real progress upstairs over the past week. These rats or mice or hamsters, or whatever they are, were in the attic all that week without anybody noticing them or coming to harm. Why don't you just ignore the little things for a couple more weeks?'

Uwe shook his head. The kids around the table stared down at their empty cups.

'I could offer you a bit more cash. Rat-money.' The workers seemed to perk up but stayed silently waiting for Uwe's orders.

There was a snapping of twigs; a muttered curse. It was Lutz, who had evidently finished unloading the van. He nodded to me; he was clenching and unclenching his fists and I noticed for the first time how the veins and knuckles stood out, like topographical features.

'Come here, Uwe,' said Lutz.

Uwe did not move. We were outside, it was cold, yet still there was a trapped intensity about our situation, as if we were convicts in a prison yard, eyeing each other for suspicious movement.

'Why, old man?'

'Because I don't believe your story about the rats. I've been looking after the house for months and there has never been any sign of rat droppings. Roof rats run across guttering. I would have noticed their crap.'

'You are calling me a liar?'

Lutz said nothing.

'What do you imagine, old man, that the rats simply came from nowhere? Go upstairs and see for yourself. That is, if you can still use your eyes.' Lutz's eyebrows were indeed wild, almost hiding his eyes.

'Just been up there,' he said. 'Part of their nest is an old milk carton – expiry date early last week. Maybe you put some rats there yourself.'

'This is ridiculous,' said Uwe turning to me, 'can't you stop this man raving?'

'All I know is, I want work to continue. It is essential for the Schloss,' I said.

'I'm not prepared to risk the health of the workers,' said Uwe.

'You will continue to work until I have investigated this rat nest properly,' I said mistaking pomposity for firmness.

'Well, you're breaking the law. We're on strike from this moment on,' declared Uwe. 'The four workers stood up, shook out the drops from their coffee cups and followed their revolutionary leader towards the Schloss. Lutz and I followed a few paces behind.

'That was a bit of a fuck-up,' I said.

'Perhaps I should have moderated my tone,' said Lutz, 'but this Uwe, he's playing a false game. He's making a fool out of you.'

'Does he want more money?'

'Maybe,' said Lutz, but he didn't seem very certain.

We passed the frog pond and moved towards the front steps of the Schloss where Uwe and his team were gathered. They were staring at a Mercedes from which two people were alighting. One wore a tightly tailored tweed jacket – the kind worn by gamblers at the horse races rather than dukes and earls – and a faintly military moustache. The other wore cargo trousers and looked to be in his late teens. He was rubbing his wrists as if steel handcuffs had just been removed, but perhaps he just had a spot of dermatitis.

'Hello,' said Harry – for it was he – 'hope I'm not interrupting anything important. This,' he said with a dramatic flourish, 'is Darren, your new master cook.' I suddenly grasped why Uwe's team were frozen to the ground. For Darren was that rare creature in the Brandenburg jungle – a black man.

Chapter 8

English Fried Bread

Lena was not the kind of woman who sobbed like an orphan at the first hint of crisis. Rather she drew up lists of problems and possible solutions; she stayed on the alert. In troubled times she would sit down, a straight-backed attentive schoolgirl, and prepare herself for awkward questions. It was like living with a yoga instructor. She even had a mat which she would unroll next to the bed; there, she would lie awake and think. I meanwhile would struggle with sleep through the night, sweating, grunting and throwing myself around the mattress. I was a wrestler; she was a mediator. I was yin; she was yang. So naturally it took me a little by surprise when she threw an admittedly ugly teapot against the admittedly unpainted wall.

'Good riddance,' I said, trying to remain nonchalant while doing up my shirt buttons. 'Not to you. I mean to the teapot. It looks as if it came from the kitchen of Imelda Marcos. Looked.' The damage, I could see, was irreparable.

Lena wandered around the room aimlessly, like a stray animal, muttering 'Shit, shit, shit.'

I wanted to put my arm around her shoulders but she shrugged me off.

'What's up?'

'You,' she said at last.

'Explain,' I said and sat on the bed. Harry and Lutz were waiting downstairs. I didn't want this to take long.

'We started this year turning over a new leaf, right? I inherited the Schloss and took it over. We decided it would be a joint project, right?'

'Yes,' I said, 'sure.' The phone rang. I picked it up, tried sensitively to switch it off, pressed the wrong button and ended up taking a photograph of my ear. On the missed calls, it said 'British Embassy'. 'Sorry,' I said, 'don't worry, I'm paying attention.'

'Are you? Here's what's wrong. This is my home, my history, my biography – and you're hijacking it. The whole bed and breakfast thing, Simon's blueprint, all those letters to the British government, Harry and his chef, the striking workers – it would have been completely unnecessary if we had just restored the house, slowly with care, rather than prostitute it.'

'Except that we wouldn't have been able to pay for it.'

'And how much are we earning at the moment? Nothing! And how much time are we spending together? Less than before! You make decisions without talking to me first and frankly they're crap decisions: you bring in that Uwe person and Lutz feels displaced and pissed off. You suck in the strangers and what happens to me? I become an irrelevance in my own ancestral home.'

I had switched the phone to vibrate and it was bumping around on the bed as if it had imbibed too much coffee. Discreetly I covered it with a pillow while studying Lena's face to inspect for tears.

Nothing. But I had rarely seen her in such a rage.

'So it's Darren that's upsetting you?'

'Not only.'

'The fact that he's black.'

'Of course not – do you think I'm some sort of racist? That would fit into your world-view perfectly, wouldn't it? The uptight German falls off her chair when she hears "Guess who's coming to dinner?"'

'Of course you wouldn't, dear. You're a woman of the world. And it's not as if you're, you know, pure German yourself.'

'Stop it!' said Lena, 'you're just digging yourself deeper into a hole! Pure German! Hah!' Her face was flushed. 'Harry should have warned us in advance. Now we have a bunch of revolutionary East German workers and a black Brit who is sure to aggravate them even more. This is Brandenburg for Christ's sake.'

'So East Germans are more likely to lynch a black than a nice Hanseatic bourgeois lady like yourself? You think this is Alabama?'

Lena slammed the door and I felt the Scandinavian timber wobble in sympathy. She was right, of course; half-right; a quarter-right. Harry should have let us know. I had taken him aside after his brief introduction of Darren.

'What's all this about?' I'd whispered.

'Darren? Good kid.' Harry seemed unperturbed.

'I thought you said he was your sister's boy. Have you got a black sister?'

'He's adopted. And he's not black. He's a mulatto.'

'You can't say that nowadays. He's mixed race. Or bi-racial. Shit, I don't know.'

'He can cook,' said Harry, 'that's all that counts.' I had known Harry a long time. At first he had been lactose-intolerant, then over the years, he had become everything-intolerant. But he had never been racist. None of us was; not Lena, not me. Was it racist to anticipate a racist reaction from someone else? After all, both Harry and I were journalists; we knew that things sometimes happened in the east, nasty things. Neo-Nazi nasty things. Asian kids hounded through town. Refugee centres set on fire. Swastikas daubed on walls. The police always called them 'isolated incidents', but a dozen 'isolated incidents' a year added up, like frequent traveller points. Anticipating possible prejudice was in itself prejudiced, I figured: it discriminated against the Ossis on the one hand, and at the same time made an issue out of Darren's colour while pretending to be colour-blind.

'I wouldn't have blinked an eyelid if he'd been my chef in England,' I'd told Harry.

'Well, stop blinking here then. You're tying yourself in knots. You liberals, you're all the same.'

The smell of fried eggs wafted towards me as I came down the staircase. I looked for evidence of Darren but it was Harry at the hob, frying up for our crisis meeting. How were we going to get the roof finished by the time the first guests appeared? We had rustled up a gang of Fontane fans as our B and B guinea pigs. They were members of the British Fontane Appreciation Society, rare creatures indeed in a country whose idea of German literature was limited to *Mein Kampf*. Britain loves its obscure clubs: admirers of tarantula spiders, philatelists who collect only blue-coloured stamps from the British Virgin Islands. The Internet had given life to these tiny tribes, linking crank with crank. So when we had announced our takeover of the Schloss on our website and hinted at a Fontane connection, some excitement was sparked among Britain's handful of *Effi Briest* admirers. Dried-up schoolteachers, mainly, who considered Effi's affair with the dashing and dangerous Major Crampas to be one of the nineteenth century's great erotic stories. Our website had been deliberately vague about the B and B's start-up date but when the Fontane groupies asked for the booking we decided to let them come. People who lived their lives vicariously through characters like Baron von Instetten, Effi's aristocratic husband, did not care about the draught in the corridor. They just wanted to breathe in the perfumed Prussian air.

Lutz was in the kitchen, in a permanent state of irritability since the hiring of Uwe; even Mac, who had adopted him and liked the smell of his jeans, was brusquely pushed away.

'Where's Darren?' I said, 'shouldn't he be cooking breakfast?'

'He's not a morning person,' said Harry, 'are you Darren?'

The boy would have looked like a man if he hadn't tried to grow a wispy nineteen-year-old's moustache on his upper lip. He was wearing the previous evening's Bob Marley T-shirt and was wiping the sleep dust from his eyes.

'Sorry, I overslept,' he said. 'Too much dope.'

We eyed him in silence, digesting the information.

'Just a joke,' he said.

'Fine,' I said doubtfully. 'Sleep well?'

'Great, man. I always sleep good with fresh air coming through the closed window.'

I ignored this reference to his undeniably draughty room.

'This is Lutz,' I said, adding – to make Darren feel more comfortable – 'He's ma man.' I had once heard Snoop Dogg say that on MTV.

To my astonishment, Lutz did not gawp at Darren like Uwe and the team.

'You from the Caribbean?' asked Lutz in his Ossi English. He was uncomfortable with verbs.

Darren nodded. 'My natural mother was from Trinidad'.

'Know it well,' said Lutz and embarked on a long, barely comprehensible account of a couple of nights that he had spent in the harbour of Port-of-Spain. Darren was listening intently but I guessed he was pretending. Before Lutz could say something really embarrassing (he was already praising the 'chocolate skin' of Trinidadian women), I tried to draw Darren back to the delicate subject of work.

'I guess you'll be doing this from now on,' I said to Darren, waving at his Uncle Harry serving up eggs on toast. 'We've got our guests coming soon, so you should be practising.'

'What's to practise?' Darren did not seem very engaged.

'Harry said food is your passion, that's right, isn't it?' Harry looked a bit disconcerted. The thought suddenly occurred to me that he had over-sold Darren's culinary skills. A potential nightmare was beginning to take shape: hole in the roof, rats, striking workers, an idle cook, a partner who was on the warpath. It could not get much worse. I was surprisingly calm. Perhaps Harry had slipped some Valium into the tea.

'I like to cook for women, you know?' said Darren. 'Make them happy, persuade them to open their mouths and swallow…'

'We get the point,' interrupted Harry. 'Darren came top of his college cooking class. And believe me he cooks for men too.'

'So tell me, what do you think are the ingredients of a perfect English breakfast, let's make sure we agree on that.' I was determined to keep Darren focussed.

'Eggs,' said Darren 'Fried, scrambled. I prefer eggs Benedict. Very sexy.'

'Cut out the sex stuff,' said Harry, 'this is breakfast. English breakfast, not a prelude to an orgy. Benedict's the Pope, right? So eggs Benedict is about filling your stomach and feeling closer to God.'

But I was beginning to see Darren's point: breakfast with eggs could be sensual despite its Englishness. Maybe we could play with this in some way. I would have to talk to Lena about it – except that Lena wasn't talking to me. I started to muse about what kind of present I could buy her as a peace offering.

'Baked beans,' Darren was continuing, 'fried bread, but fried in olive oil. Beef rather than pork sausages. Grilled tomatoes. Crispy bacon, very thin.'

'Can you be sensual and healthy?' I said, asking myself rather than Darren. 'Or do you need a bit of decadence?'

'Butter is decadent,' said Harry, 'use lots of it.'

'I prefer olive oil. And I don't serve cheese.'

'Well, if a guest wanted cheese, you would serve it up I hope.'

'No, I wouldn't,' said Darren. 'That's the way I do things. That's the deal.'

A bit presumptuous for a nineteen-year-old, I thought. The deal, after all, was that he was getting a free room – albeit the coldest and dampest in the house – and I paid him pocket money and kept him out of the sights of the British police for a while. That was a pretty good arrangement in return for cooking a bit of breakfast and helping out in the Schloss. But I didn't say anything out loud in case he got the wrong idea and thought I was anti-black or anti-brown or whatever.

'Right, you've passed the Breakfast IQ test,' said Harry, wiping egg yolk from his Hemingway moustache. 'What we have to decide now is a strategy – where's Lena by the way?'

'Thought you might know.'

Harry looked at me strangely.

'She marched out of the house before you came down,' said Harry, 'looked as if she was about to shoot something.'

'Or somebody,' I chipped in.

Lutz, not quite keeping up with the pace of conversation, added his fifty cents of wisdom:

'It's very difficult to shoot things at this time of year. There are strict rules.'

'Really?' said Harry. 'In England we just kill any animal that gets on our nerves. Which brings me to point one. If we are going to get your roof fixed quickly then first we have to get rid of the bloody rats or whatever they are. No rats – no reasons for workers to moan. Second, someone has to go and talk them back into working. And that someone shouldn't be Lutz – who will exterminate them even without a licence – and it shouldn't be you.' I nodded in agreement.

'That leaves you,' I said.

'Yeah, I suppose it does. I can be the emissary from our generation to the young-scrounger, pay-me-for-doing-nothing generation. The Germans love their Council of Elders, their Helmut Schmidts, right? They still believe age brings wisdom, don't they? I'll sort these kids out.'

'Old you certainly are, Uncle Harry,' said Darren with a hint of mockery, as if doubting the wisdom bit.

'Listen, I'm so old that I was addicted to pornography even before the Internet was invented. That's how old I am.'

'I don't believe that, Uncle, you always respect women.' Harry and I stared at Darren, trying to work out whether he was being ironic. Always difficult to tell with the younger generation.

'Your task, Darren, since you missed your cooking duties this morning,' said Harry, taking charge – indeed almost relieving me of command – 'is to solve the vermin problem in the attic.'

'No problem, Uncle.' Darren stood up and tugged a carving knife out of the open cutlery drawer. He ran his finger lightly over the blade. 'That should do it,' he said.

'No cruelty, Darren,' I called after him as he half-ran up the stairs, weightless as a fox. 'Lena won't stand for it.'

I did not need unnecessary complications with Lena.

She was outside: my chance to make amends to show that I was really interested in her. Lena had discovered a segment of soil that could be used to grow vegetables and had decided that Darren should serve up organic food. There had been some light rain so the earth was less caked than usual and Lena was trowelling hard.

'Ah,' I said, breathing in with theatrical vigour. 'What fine air! I'm looking forward to having strangers in the house!' That was my way of reminding Lena that she would soon need to pin on a smile and act as a charming hostess. She didn't look up.

'What are you planting?' I wasn't much of a gardener. To me, it seemed as if she was completing one of those pointless tasks that you get given in the army: like digging a hole in order to fill another, or whitewashing lumps of coal.

Lena glared at me.

'Pineapples,' she said.

'Aha,' I said, and guessed that this was a woman's way of telling me that since I had no idea about gardening, she had a licence to treat me as a fool. 'That's nice.'

While she dug up weeds, I lit up a cigarette. For some reason this also seemed to annoy her and I tried to fill the angry silence with a short monologue on Theodor Fontane.

'So it would be really good,' I concluded, 'if you could show the guests around – because you're the only German in the house. Not counting Lutz, of course. And Harry and I are really busy at the moment.'

Wordlessly she stripped off her gloves and went indoors. What was I doing wrong?

'Just saw your Lena stomping upstairs,' said Harry who, having set up a dartboard on one of the kitchen cupboards, was practising for a game against Darren. 'I expect she was going to clean herself up a bit. What's got into her?'

'Don't know,' I said, 'she seems to think that we're excluding her from the plans for the house.'

'Ridiculous,' said Harry.

'Women,' said Lutz, 'they're difficult.'

'Sex brings us together, gender drives us apart,' said Harry.

An hour later Lena dutifully appeared, scrubbed clean of make-up, hair tied back, and a prim dress that buttoned to her neck. It was her Amish look and I was tempted to ask whether she was heading for a prayer meeting. Instead I gave a sensitive smile and held my tongue. We both knew that before we could take in guests, we needed a seal of approval from the British Embassy. The ambassador, no doubt hoping to thwart us, was sending a controller to the Schloss to judge how fast work was progressing. That was the condition of receiving subsidies from the British government: a Schloss that was grand enough to demonstrate the full splendour of British culture to the Ossi. And a Lord and Lady of the Manor who could demonstrate an easy familiarity not just with German literature before and after the Goebbels Diaries, but also Shakespeare, Chaucer and the usual British geniuses.

We had, in short, to be culturally bi-lingual, masters of the Anglo-German relationship. I hoped that Lena would be on her best behaviour and wouldn't spoil things by throwing crockery around. There were few sins as profound in the Anglican credo as smashing a teapot in anger. Lena looked thoughtful, stroked the back of her neck, but did not return my encouraging smile.

When the controller came, he brought with him the smell of burning wood and the great outdoors. It was, I knew, the trademark scent of an expensive aftershave that could be bought only in London's Jermyn Street.

'Arbuthnot de Villiers, Cultural and Citizenship Issues' is what was written on his business card and I could see straight away that Arbuthnot inhabited a different world. He was a typical third son. The English nobility laid great store on producing male offspring. The firstborn was doomed to inherit, which usually meant inheriting debts. It was for Number One Son to sell off old paintings to pay the fuel bills for seventy-roomed country castles. The second-born went into the army, his salary supplemented by income from the estate. And the third son?

He became a priest or joined the Foreign Office. Sooner or later he would become a bishop or an ambassador or, if he got lucky, the demise of his father would be followed by the rapid death of his older brothers and he would become Lord of the Manor. Then he too could take on the task of selling the family treasures and sacking the butler. It was not a good time to be an aristocrat.

They have a special manner, these third sons, a languid acceptance that their future is not really in their hands; that there is no point in trying to build a supersonic career. Third sons are not ambitious: like everyone stuck in a waiting room, they look for distraction.

Arbuthnot de Villiers was, it seemed, in favour of our Schloss.

'I like the dartboard,' he said, 'good touch. A great British sport.' Harry had forgotten to take it down before rushing out of the house. As promised, he had arranged a negotiating session with Uwe and the workers. It was a relief to have him out of the way; it gave Lena a free hand to explain the – her – Schloss to the diplomat.

'We're not completely ready,' said Lena, 'it's a bit higgledy-piggledy.' An old-fashioned English word, a children's nursery word, designed to appeal to emotionally retarded members of Britain's former ruling class.

'Higgledy-piggledy? That's the way it should be,' said Arbuthnot, unfolding his long limbs in the best of the living-room chairs. He must have been in his mid thirties but was dressed in Harris Tweed, which immediately aged a man by fifteen years. I waited for him to take out a pipe.

'May I?' He stuffed it with tobacco as if loading a waste incinerator. I waited for him to light up and skunk up the place. The smell of my own cigarettes I liked – it was, after all, my smell. But pipes? Nein Danke. Yet Arbuthnot did not spark a match. Instead, he just left it uncombusted, a cocked gun, a weapon to be used only in emergency. Arbuthnot de Villiers, I realised, was that special kind of man: the passive-aggressive, recently converted non-smoker.

'I grew up in an old pile' – a euphemism probably for an Edwardian building with a tennis court in the grounds – 'so I know the problems.'

'The cold bedrooms,' I volunteered.

'The damp,' added Lena. 'The draughts.'

'Exactly,' said Arbuthnot, 'the true spirit of the English country house.'

'Except that this is a little Prussian Schloss,' said Lena.

'Quite.' Arbuthnot de Villiers waited for us to elaborate, fiddling dangerously with his still-unlit pipe.

'These Prussian houses were meeting places,' said Lena. 'It must have been very difficult to get around the region in the nineteenth century. So when people come to stay they did so for a minimum of two nights. And depending on the visitors there would be an intellectual salon, or a musical evening. I think they were mainly places for men to meet women.'

'A kind of aristo-disco,' I said.

'A striking image,' said Arbuthnot.

'And that was my – our – idea,' continued Lena, 'to place the house in a modern context. Only in our case, to bring the English and the Prussians together. Which is why we have concentrated on the downstairs salon.'

She was right to be proud. Everything about the living room encouraged the huddling together of strangers curious about each other: the stove, the open kitchen, the long dining table, the delicately lit corners. It was the style known as Shabby Chic.

The last time that the British were chic was in the early nineteenth century when the whole of Europe copied dandies like Beau Brummell, established men's clubs and even experimented a bit with democracy. Annoyed that everybody was copying us, we chose to look as run-down as possible. Men wore their shirts until they frayed; sofas were allowed to become ragged and smell of dog; books sprawled everywhere in the house. The logic was this: some things are so beautiful or useful they should not be hidden, but rather scattered around the house. The German way was to conceal the old and time-worn; our way was to celebrate the shabby.

'That sounds to be on the right track,' said the diplomat, brushing ash from his waistcoat. 'The government certainly thinks so.' He broke off at the sight of Darren coming down the stairs, clutching a plastic bag heading for the kitchen.

'Darren,' I said, 'come and shake hands with Mr De Villiers. Darren is our chef, hired specially to re-invent the English breakfast.'

'Arbuthnot,' said Arbuthnot, and held out his hand.

Darren stared at it, contemplating perhaps how he could remove the diplomat's signet ring without him noticing.

'I do approve,' said Arbuthnot, in an almost bedroom whisper so that Darren couldn't hear him while he made some milky tea for the diplomat. 'You are putting the face of modern Britain on display. Multicultural, young, innovative cooking – is that a sushi knife he's washing? – I'm sure my superiors will approve.' Darren dried his hands and, out of view of the diplomat, gave me a thumbs-up sign as if to say: mission accomplished. We were rat-free. But what had he actually done with the rodents? I hoped that there hadn't been a bloodbath in the attic.

'There are just a few formalities to be sorted out,' said Arbuthnot, opening his battered brown leather briefcase and removing a sheaf of papers. 'Now, in order to qualify for the government's cultural ambassadorship scheme, that is to become a "Gold Champion"' – Arbuthnot winced at the term that had obviously been devised by an expensive advertising PR company in an attempt to rebrand stuffy British foreign policy – 'you have to answer some questions correctly.'

I dreaded this. My head had been stuffed – like Lutz's – with dead knowledge. So-called 'mental arithmetic', the solving of $9 \times 9 \times 23$ in one's head – a superfluous exercise which could be solved a hundred times quicker by using an electronic calculator. The spelling of long, obscure words that could be ascertained by spellcheck on the computer. Or geography which had been replaced by GPS; or history by Wikipedia. I had learned so much, forgotten more – I didn't need to be cross-examined by a young man in a tweed jacket. But that, it seemed, was the price for British government support.

'OK,' said Arbuthnot, 'which document established the rights of the British parliament: A. the Mappa Mundi, B. the Magna Carta or C. the Bill of Rights?'

'B,' I said, astonished that my redundant knowledge was indeed being demanded, 'in 1215.'

'Correct,' said Arbuthnot, making a tick. 'Let's skip history. Here's the serious stuff. Breakfast knowledge. White bread, whole grain or rye?'

'White, of course,' I replied, quick as a flash.

'Correct,' Arbuthnot made a tick.

'Bacon, greasy or lean?'

'Greasy.'

'Correct.'

'Porridge with salt or honey?'

'Salt.'

'Correct.'

'Tell me,' I said, 'are you asking us the right questions? Aren't they part of the British Citizenship Test?'

Arbuthnot shuffled through his papers, dropping some on the floor.

'Good God,' he said, 'you're right. Got the question sheets mixed up. Can't ask you these – what if you get some wrong, we'd have to strip you of your citizenship. That would be a bad thing, what?' A dry joke from Arbuthnot.

'You could always let Lena answer them and make her an honorary citizen,' I suggested.

'Only way you can do that nowadays, old chap, is to marry her.'

Lena reddened, with anger rather than embarrassment.

'I would like to remind you two gentlemen that I am actually present in this room and am not a block of wood.'

'Quite, quite,' said Arbuthnot, suddenly serious. 'Good point.'

The correct questions were equally obscure – how to greet the Queen, the right amount of milk to put into tea, decent behaviour in the queue for Wimbledon, the first name of the Archbishop of Canterbury – but Lena answered them all without flinching.

'Well, that's it,' said Arbuthnot. 'I think it's fair to say that you will soon be Culture Champions. The government requires you, in return for your monthly cheque, to fly the British flag over the house. The German flag is optional, but we would prefer you not to. It might confuse the natives. You will also be required to extend the reach of Britain into the local community.'

'Meaning?'

'Meaning, for example, Highland dancing to celebrate the poet Rabbie Burns' birthday. Perhaps you could get your charming Darren to cook a haggis. Or you could offer classes to the locals on how to make the perfect cup of tea. If you had a field you could organise a polo match. Something physical, the Germans have loved all that stuff since all their nineteenth-century Body Culture stuff. Up to you. Remember it's compulsory. No culture, no cash, I'm afraid.'

'We'll let you know,' I said. 'We'll get our Events Manager on the job.' Meaning Harry.

'By tomorrow,' said Arbuthnot who had now dropped all pretence of being a laid-back English gentleman, 'or the cheque might not go through.'

I showed Arbuthnot to his Range Rover and, relieved to have him out of the way, lit up a cigarette. It had gone well, I thought. Normally I would now have had a glass of wine with Lena to analyse the meeting, like football players after a big match. But now, with Lena's nerves so frayed, I doubted that we would do more than exchange a few words. Harry had assured me that the moment would pass. 'PMT,' he said, knowingly. 'Pre-menstrual tension. The cause of eighty per cent of the world's wars.' I pondered this for a while. 'Afghanistan?' I said, dubiously remembering the burkas and stoned adulteresses. 'Especially there.'

My thought processes, perhaps not quite as deep as they should have been, were interrupted by raised voices, the banging of pans, the sharp retort of a smashed plate. In the kitchen, Darren and Lena were yelling at each other. Lena was turning beetroot red and Darren was, well, black. I sidled in and moved the carving knives safely out of their grasp. One of the knives had a spot of blood and I guessed the problem.

'I told you not to kill the rats,' I said to Darren.

'I didn't kill them!'

Lena glared at Darren, and then at me.

'So what's this?' I held up the knife.

'My blood, I pricked myself.'

'He's put the rats in a cage and wants to make them into a miniature circus,' said Lena, almost spitting with outrage. It must have been like this in her ancestral Italian kitchen, full of passion and hand-waving and operatic beating of ample chests.

'Darren, you can't do that! We're not the Addams Family! This is supposed to be as pure and sterile as a restaurant kitchen.'

'They're OK, rats. We have them at home in Brixton. Look, Uncle Harry promised me that if I get lonely here I could have a pet. What do you think it feels like here, no friends, no gin, no nothing.' There was, of course, a long history of prisoners training rats or pigeons, which, after all, were just rats with wings. Perhaps Darren saw himself as Brandenburg's Birdman of Alcatraz. I started to feel a little sorry for him.

Lena, however, did not.

'The rats have got to go!' she said.

Darren removed one gently from the cage, which he had left on the floor next to a crate of cheap wine that we had bought for the Fontane fans. It was surprisingly passive in his hands as if it was used to being stroked by cooks in the kitchen.

'Let him go at once!' commanded Lena. By which she no doubt meant: put the rodent back in its cage. Darren however took the order literally and let the rat drop to the floor. It landed with an easy grace.

'Stop the bloody thing escaping,' I said and moved clumsily forward, thinking I could catch the animal with my bare hands, while it was still in shock. All I succeeded in doing though was kicking the cage. The door opened and Darren's favourite rat was joined by five others. All six started to scurry fast around the salon, jumping on the sofa, catching on the curtains. After weeks in a cold damp attic they must have thought that they had died and gone to rat-paradise.

'Catch them, for God's sake,' said Lena.

I grabbed a broom and Darren snatched an ancient Persian cashmere cover from the sofa. Without discussing a plan we had instinctively assumed the role of a gladiatorial team: me pushing the rats with the broom towards a spot where Darren could smother them with cashmere. Then what? Beat them to death? Stuff them into a bag and take them outside?

Lena wasn't waiting for a resolution to this ethical problem. Just as Darren and I covered one of his would-be pets, we heard the door slam. Lena had walked out.

Fair Play

Only on the next day, waking up in a bed that was fifty per cent cold, did I realise that Lena had not just staged a brief tactical withdrawal. She had gone and, since the Opel had disappeared, I could only assume that she was bunkering down in Berlin. Harry advised me against ringing her. First, he suggested, let her calm down. And catch the last fugitive rat. Even before making breakfast, Darren had taken the other captured rats – the Globnitz Five as Harry insisted on calling them – and released them in the church graveyard. I did not really subscribe to Harry's Stone Age theories about PMT, nor was I aware of Lena having a long-standing allergy to rats. She did however seem to be allergic to Darren. What was going on, I figured, was an undeclared struggle for the beating heart of the Schloss: the kitchen. Initially, it seemed as if Lena was all in favour of having someone else doing the cooking. Her ambition, after all, was to be a Lady of the Manor in the old-fashioned way. But Darren was perhaps a little too innovative – or a little too much Harry's idea. There was something stirring deep within Lena, but I couldn't work it out.

'How can women expect men to understand them if they don't supply subtitles?' I asked Harry.

He shrugged.

'They just don't grasp how much we have to deal with,' he said. 'Getting up every day, putting on our trousers, using a knife and fork, taking the dog for a walk.'

The classic recipe for incomprehension is to wallow in work. This time it didn't really help. Why should it? Work isn't a substitute for thought; if it were it would be more popular. Darren had insisted that his breakfast eggs be organic so, to humour him – and because mysteriously we had some wood left over from our IKEA adventure – Lutz and I began to build a fox-proof hen coop in the garden. Bit by bit the garden was beginning to resemble the kind of practical allotment that people in the West were advised to build in the 1950s. Four simple lessons for surviving atomic war: 1. Construct a shelter. 2. Prepare to grow your own vegetables. 3. Breed chickens. 4. Buy a shotgun to defend your land from survivors who have not been as prudent as you.

Days passed without contact from Lena and so the memory of Darren's rats receded. Mac had discovered the last missing rodent and dealt with him in the usual canine way. Together, without Lena, we settled into an all-male routine. Lutz and Darren were getting on just fine. The old man taught him how to saw wood, drill holes and make a shed for egg-producers. Darren had brought his ghetto blaster sound system (called, for obvious reasons, something quite different in German) and played Bob Marley at earth-shaking volume: 'No Woman, No Cry'. Well, it was not difficult to apply the lyrics to my situation. No Lena, no sense. We were gripped by a collective feeling of abandonment. The captain had abruptly left the ship.

'What's all this about?' asked Harry.

'Beats me,' I said. 'You know – women.'

But for once my appeal to male solidarity didn't seem to wash with my cheerleader-in-chief. His grimace said plainly: you're messing up.

The whole purpose of the Schloss was to find a common dream but, judging by Lena's outburst and démarche, it looked as if we were growing apart even faster than when we were both working in demanding jobs. The collective brainpower of the Schloss had dramatically dropped. Harry still had his journalist's instinctive cunning; Darren his street-wisdom; Lutz his Made-in-the-DDR gift for improvisation. Somehow, though, when we were together in the evenings, men of three different generations, our conversational level seemed to sink to the level of a Saturday night in an average London pub, just after the football highlights had been shown on TV. Harry was the first to realise it.

'This isn't going to work without Lena,' he said, as we threw darts, with declining concentration, at the board in the kitchen.

'Get the woman back,' agreed Lutz.

'That's easier said than done,' I said, thinking of the arrival of the Fontane fans in only four days. 'There's so much to do here before the guests come.'

'No there isn't, it's all in hand,' said Harry. Even allowing for his perpetual bouncy optimism, Harry did have a point. His negotiating tactics with the work team had brought results. Instead of going straight to Uwe as the informal group leader, he had gone to each of the four workers individually and offered them ten per cent more cash in hand. The alternative, he suggested, might be sudden and unexpected death. With his big fat Mercedes, clipped moustache and Burberry trench coat, he probably came over as more credible than me, with my worn out duffel coat and retro-chic Humana jeans. Once the boys had agreed to come back, Uwe had no choice but to join them. All the team had to do now was to patch up the roof with something temporary, and pretty the place up. Some more flower tubs, that kind of thing.

There was nothing stopping me going to Berlin for a day and trying to sort out our problems. Lena had taken the Opel and I wanted Harry to stay in the Schloss to keep an eye on the workers and on Darren. So I took the train and trundled through the countryside, which was changing colour, from grey to khaki. Spring was coming; a German spring, slow but thorough. There was never a sudden shock of daffodils, not here in the north-east. Rather the shift in seasons was like an accumulation of small clues at a crime scene. Bushes became leafy enough to hide rubbish bags under the branches; crocuses cropped up among the dog droppings; the sun was briefly strong enough to expose smeared windows. Even Mac, tucked under the seat lest the inspector demand a ticket, was a shade more frisky, in need of female companionship. Better than the work crew in the Schloss – who were, after all, mere human males – he sensed there was something wrong, the absence of his mistress. As early as Köpenick, passengers started to shift their luggage, impatient to reach the city, the brightness of it all; it was as if the few kilometres had transported them from the nineteenth to the twenty-first century and they were terrified that if they did not get off in time, the full force of chaotic German history would knock them senseless. For me though, Berlin seemed like a step backwards in personal time. In Brandenburg I was making something happen; in Berlin very few people made anything at all. After a few weeks away, Berlin had come to seem like a convalescent city, the German patient. The mayor of Berlin had once tried to put a good shine on the place by calling it 'poor but sexy'. By which he meant: the capital was becoming as compellingly interesting for outsiders as it had been in the 1920s, in the days of decadent cabarets. Then, tough, gritty Berlin had factories cranking out everything from sewing machines to light bulbs. There was an air of bustling prosperity, of ringing cash machines. The sense of industry underpinned the creative process. Now a quarter of the city was on the dole, even more on welfare benefits – and the sound of the city was distinguished rather by the loud mid-morning snore, the fitful zzzzzz, of young people recovering from yet another pointless night on the tiles. Poor yes; sexy no.

Yet Lena, angry, had dashed back to the city. It occurred to me that although the Schloss belonged to Lena, she was less committed to it than I was. She had expressed it differently in her outburst, made it seem as if I had stolen an idea from her. But perhaps it was simply this: she was falling out of love with the Schloss. Or, worse, her love for me was ebbing and the Schloss had somehow become a symbol of our relationship – an untidy building site full of noise and unsolved problems. Both relationships and home renovations needed a degree of faith. Hers was wavering, mine had somehow grown stronger.

I couldn't afford the taxi so I took the S-Bahn to the Grunewald apartment we could no longer afford. During the journey I thought: I must tell Lena my fears. There is, after all, no voodoo curse on those who break silence about relationships.

Ours had taken a conventional route. If you pulled out the photos from our memory box you would find breakfasts and dinners, holidays with sunburns, waking up together, walking across puddles, and always talk, talk, talk. What we hadn't had was an adventure, an expedition into the jungle. That was what we were having now. And Lena had run away. It did not seem fair. I needed an explanation.

No one answered the door. Nothing had changed, but I sensed that she had been and gone. Perhaps to collect some clothes, or some cosmetics. She had left the Schloss abruptly, taking almost nothing. In the flat everything was in its appointed place and yet shifted slightly in the sly manner that cleaning ladies use to tell their female bosses that a surface has been wiped clean. But of course we no longer had a cleaning lady. Our unspoken thought about the Grunewald apartment, despite all its sunlight and custom-made bookshelves, was that we would not be returning there; that we were making our pact with the countryside.

Lena could be with one of three possible friends. Or with her mother in Hamburg. I tried the friends, left email and text messages. She did not pick up the phone. I did not try her mother, who was on the surface a generous-hearted welcoming woman but who, when her vital interests appeared to be under challenge, resembled the kind of ice pick that was used to kill Leon Trotsky. Instead, I scribbled a note:

'Lena, dearest, I am searching for you. There's some misunderstanding. I know there is room in our lives for each other – and for the bloody Schloss. If you read this call me – I kiss you.'

I deliberately made the handwriting seem unsteady, as if I were writing in the white-hot glow of passion whereas in fact I had spent thirty minutes thinking about how many kisses I should sign off with. Maybe she would get back to me that day, maybe not. In the meantime, I had to stay in control of the affairs of the Schloss.

Simon, fortunately, did answer his phone. We agreed to meet at Café Brel that evening in Savignyplatz.

'Who'd have thought it,' he snorted as he found my table in the back room, 'a café named after a famous Belgian.' It was dedicated to the singer Jacques Brel, played his caustic self-pitying songs, and had hung up black-and-white pictures of his ugly handsome face.

'Tintin,' I said, 'Audrey Hepburn. All Belgians. I thought you were in the nation-branding business.'

'You're very stroppy. And you look even worse than usual.'

'Woman trouble,' I said. 'I feel misunderstood. She feels misunderstood.'

'Then you should get married,' said Simon, 'and have misunderstood children. But you probably didn't want to talk sex with me?'

'No, even worse – about the embassy. They are demanding an events calendar before they sign the cheques. Apparently they won't be satisfied until the English can be seen having physical contact with the East Germans.'

'Let's have mussels to eat. The Belgians are good on molluscs.' Simon waved at the waiter, sipped a non-Belgian wine and thought for a moment.

'What you have to do,' he said, 'is capture the sense of fair play. The Germans think this encapsulates everything positive about the British. Curling on the ice, golf on the green, policemen who say 'please' and 'thank you'. That's what you're supposed to do out there in the bush.'

I thought of the only time that I had ever played golf with Harry, and how he had hidden my ball in the long grass.

'Yes,' I said doubtfully, 'though I'm not sure we do smiling policemen anymore.'

'Well, you could try golf,' said Simon. 'Great tradition. Do you have any suitable putting green?'

'Just the old Soviet barracks,' I said, 'where they used to practise artillery fire in preparation for the invasion of Dortmund.'

'Won't do,' said Simon glumly, brightening up however as the plates of mussels were plonked in front of us. They were piled up high and I couldn't imagine eating my way through so much Flemish marine life. My worry about Lena had contracted my stomach, chewed it up.

'For God's sake, don't worry about overeating,' said Simon, spotting my reluctance. 'Overeating is the most worthy of sins – it doesn't break up marriages, it doesn't cause car crashes.' He patted his stomach. Then, with a gasp: 'I've got it!'

'What? Colic?'

'No – cricket! You should organise a cricket match!'

This didn't strike me as worthy of a eureka moment.

'Germans are no good with bat and ball,' I told him. 'Sure they can connect their feet with balls. Tennis rackets and balls, yes. There are a few tall Germans who can put balls into nets, or use their hands to knock them over nets. But bat and ball, no.'

Simon looked surprised that I had not jumped up from the table and embraced him.

'They knock down skittles,' he said, somewhat huffily.

I remembered the bowling alley in the basement of Gundi's pub; the slow grunt that Horst would emit when he released his oversized ball. The absurd triumph of hitting immobile, unprotected chunks of wood barely 20 metres away. A chimpanzee could succeed at bowling, and that was the point; it was a game with a lower skill rating than Ludo. Hence its popularity in America.

'Bowling is for losers,' I said. Although, on reflection, I had enjoyed the mock-seriousness of playing against Horst and other members of the Voluntary Fire Brigade. Like it or not, I was becoming one of them: an Alt-Globnitzer. A loser.

'And cricket isn't?' retorted Simon. 'Eleven men on one team, who spend most of their time waiting to pick up a bat. Eleven on the other team with ten of them standing around waiting to catch a ball if it happens to fly in their direction.'

I was a little surprised by Simon's insight. I had him down as a cricket patriot who believed in the sanctity of the national game.

'The point about cricket, its political point, was to explain the principle of boredom to non-Christian members of the British Empire,' said Simon. 'In the end everyone is so overcome by the inactivity and sheer mass of inexplicable rules that they don't care who wins or who loses – and that is the definition of fair play. It's how we civilised half the world.'

'Afghanistan,' I said, nodding my head enthusiastically.

'Great cricketers,' confirmed Simon, 'great bat-to-ball co-ordination.'

'And now...'

'Brandenburg, yes!' Simon drew a notepad out of his pocket and started to scribble. 'We'll get the press to come, even if they are hyenas… oh, sorry,' he said, glancing up at me, 'keep forgetting you're a journalist.'

'Me too,' I said, and checked my phone. No message from Lena.

'What you have to do is organise eleven local players, doesn't matter what age, train them to play, find a pitch, and lay on some planter's punch for the spectators. I suspect your friend, er…'

'Harry.'

'Harry. He could fix that. I can scratch together an England side to play your lot. Maybe we can get a pseudo-silver cup and call it something like the Schloss Alt-Globnitz Annual Anglo-German Tournament. Let's give it a bit of time – we will need a bit of green to appear in Brandenburg. And it will be difficult to make a proper team out of that Ossi rabble.'

'Hey!' I said. 'They're all right. Most of them.' Lutz, I thought. Horst, even Reckless Robert. They all had their lives messed up by dictators and came out OK.

'Going native already, eh? We'll soon be seeing you in those ridiculous trousers.'

'Jogging pants, you mean. They're very comfortable. Elasticated waists.'

Simon rolled his eyes.

'No wonder Lena's left you,' he said, 'you've let yourself go.'

I stood up, nodded curtly, put some cash on the table, said 'thanks' and strode to the exit. Had Lena really left me?

From Café Brel to Bahnhof Zoo it was a short, miserable walk. A grizzled tramp scaring away a young man with a full bladder from using the Savignyplatz toilet; it was early evening and already he was marking out plainly the place he intended to spend the night. Turning the corner past the Beate Uhse sex shop: the smell of detergent wafting out of the video cabins. Two kids furtively exchanging packets presumably full of amphetamines. The station, free of dealers but not the mentally ill. A woman with a grey coat that touched her ankles and Medusa-like hair started to wail like a foghorn. Two policemen moved toward her.

'Leave her alone,' I said. 'She's just unhappy. That's not illegal.'

'Yeah, she's just rehearsing for Pop Idol,' said some smart-ass kid on a bench.

The police shrugged and went for a coffee.

The S-Bahn took me to the Hauptbahnhof. From the grimy window I saw some shivering giraffes in the zoo and thought: poor bastards, so far from home. I rang Arbuthnot on the mobile. 'That's a great idea, yes, cricket and fair play. Excellent. Very British. No one uses steroids or anything in cricket nowadays, do they? It's got to be a clean sport, you see, no bike-riders or sprinters. Otherwise the project will all go wrong, you see?'

I assured him that the local team would be as innocent as choirboys, as honest as boy scouts, as drug-free as Angela Merkel. The Vatican itself would not be able to produce as upright a team as Alt-Globnitz. Just as long as the embassy came up with its cheque.

'It's in the post, old boy,' he said. 'The deal is as good as done.'

Thinking about Lena, nothing but Lena. Would it help if I sacked Darren? I strode through the main foyer of the station. The last train to Alt-Globnitz was due to depart within minutes. Or at least I thought so: the station had been designed like an airport and had therefore banished clocks. Its sole purpose was to persuade passengers to spend more money in the shopping mall and lose their sense of time. If that meant missing their train, well, so be it. Even more time available to shop. Suddenly, just ahead of me, I spotted a familiar figure – the small but top-heavy muscular structure of the esteemed mayor of Alt-Globnitz. He was wearing a hat, perhaps the only person in the whole station to be doing so, and I could only assume that he wanted to make himself look taller or hide thinning hair. He had a small wheeled case (why don't men carry their bags anymore? – have their vertebrae collapsed?) and a rolled-up newspaper. When I approached him he looked embarrassed as if caught in a solitary sex act.

'Herr Bürgermeister,' I shouted as if greeting an old friend from Texas, 'are you returning to your electorate?'

'Ah,' he said, and promptly sprayed his throat with some kind of anti-bacterial spray. 'I've just arrived. I'm on town business. Talks with investors.'

He said this so quickly, so nervously, that I immediately assumed he had an appointment with an escort girl. Oddly, this made him more sympathetic. Why not tell him about the cricket match, I thought, get him involved.

But before I could broach the subject, he said abruptly: 'Hear you've solved your labour dispute. Work back on schedule.

Good news.' He sprayed again. I hadn't even attempted to shake his hand, knowing that this would require the use of surgical sterile rubber gloves.

'Yes,' I said, wanting to raise the question of Uwe, his brother-in-law, to get to the bottom of his furtiveness. Two men however were walking towards us, their heels digging into the floor. One, pinch-faced, in newly ironed Dolce and Gabbana jeans; all in black. Russian. The other: scuffed shoes, a barrel chest, shiny suit stretched tight. Nationality unclear. He was the one who spoke, with a hint of an accent. It could have been Italian – but an Italian with unpolished shoes? With a shirt collar that curled up?

'The car's waiting,' he said. The mayor's right hand rose and fell like the barrier on a railway crossing. I understood the gesture. It meant: under normal circumstances I might have considered shaking your hand but there are too many germs in a railway station. So please be content with a half-wave. Slightly mystified by the rest of the mayor's behaviour – who would supply a car and what looked like a bodyguard to pick up a mayor from a tiny East German community – I rushed to the platform to catch the last train home.

It is a cliché of the love war that women, at unhappy moments in their relationship, wait for the telephone to ring. Conveniently placed near the paper handkerchiefs and a bowl of Häagen-Dazs chocolate chip ice cream, the phone may not actually be answered when it rings, but it does form part of the ritual of break-up. Misery measured by the number of missed calls. Less obvious is the fact that men too hug their phones in moments of separation. True, they switch the phone to silent and leave it in the pocket of a coat. But throughout the working day, they find excuses to check for messages; fifteen minutes' concentration is the most that can be expected from a man in this situation.

And Lena did not call. Almost four days – ninety-two hours to be precise – had passed since the row between Lena and Darren and she might as well have been kidnapped and taken for interrogation at a clandestine CIA base; she was incommunicado, swallowed into a cosmic void. There had been plenty to distract me, to keep the Schloss team busy: the scaffolding had to be taken down from the front of the house – the roof had been plugged and given a makeshift insulation, the garden made passingly attractive, the last of the furniture assembled, sheets put on beds, plumbing checked, matching towels laid out, Darren's provisions stocked up. Above all, we had to present ourselves as experts on Effi Briest. I had prepared a checklist of characters. Each of us would take on the identity of one of Fontane's protagonists and take the guests around the Mark. Harry had decided that he should be the unreliable Major Crampas. I, for some reason, was supposed to reveal the world of dried-up Baron von Instetten. Lutz had grudgingly agreed to act out the part of Effi's father. Lena, though darker than Effi, had originally agreed to role-play as Fontane's heroine. The plan had been to take the group on horseback and gallop them across fields, wind in their faces, just as Effi had done. Without Lena, it was difficult to see how we were going to manage this charade.

'Maybe we could just take them all to Tropical Island,' muttered Harry. He was referring to a heated swimming pool complex in Brandenburg where entrepreneurs had once – in the heady days after unification – tried to build a new kind of Zeppelin that had gone bankrupt. Now the same huge assembly hall was being used to bring the Caribbean experience to the East: sand, deckchairs, overpriced rum cocktails, frites smothered in mayonnaise, floating on the water. It did not sound like the ideal destination for serious, scholarly fans of the great Theodor Fontane.

Lutz interrupted his study of the Briest book; I had underlined the key phrases with a yellow marker pen and all Lutz really had to do was point out the local beauty spots to our enthusiastic paying guests and read out a few sentences. But Lutz was not a reading man and thought the whole idea was ridiculous. He slammed the book shut.

'This won't work,' he said with an air of finality. 'The guided tours, all that stuff. It can't happen without Lena. She is the woman of the house. Only she,' – he slapped the cover of the book – 'can make all that stuff interesting.'

Harry, I could see, did not want to be openly disloyal and stayed silent.

'Let's not worry about this now,' Harry said at last. We stood up and looked out into the gloom. The bus with the Fonty-tourists was long overdue; against Lutz's better judgement we had let Uwe take a rented minibus to collect them from Schönefeld airport. They would be tired and hungry after flying cattle-class on easyJet. Darren had agreed to make them dinner. Perhaps with full stomachs, they would – like most British tourists – become docile. We turned to inspect the salon one last time and tried to see it through Lena's eyes. Wilting flowers! Coffee mugs on the table! An ashtray with three stubbed-out cigarettes. The others helped me whisk round; the *Putztruppe* from Prussia. Harry lit some candles; Darren took Bob Marley out of the CD player and slipped in Louis Armstrong's 'What a Wonderful World'. By the time the bus shuddered to a halt, even Mac was looking pretty.

With the air of tired soldiers, the six tourists (one had cancelled because of flu) collected their luggage from the back and stared up at the house. Uwe seemed to be smirking. Something told me that he had taken the long way from the airport. But they had arrived now and it was a pleasure to see the stress of bargain-travel slip from their rounded shoulders. We ushered them in and the aroma of Darren's cooking – he had decided to make liver and onions – swept over them.

'Welcome to Schloss Alt-Globnitz,' said Harry, embarking on the speech I should have made. 'You have the honour of being the first guests in the place since the fall of communism. You'll find that the countryside at least hasn't changed much since Fontane explored the place.'

Harry introduced me as co-owner with Lena, who had sadly been called away on a family emergency. 'Thanks for giving me a mention,' I hissed into Harry's ear.

'If I'd waited for you to collect your thoughts we wouldn't have heard from you until Fonty's two-hundredth birthday,' replied Harry. And to show he had done a little bit of research, he added, 'in 2019'.

The group, it seemed, was just relieved to be in the warmth. Two of the men wore green fishermen's vests with lots of pockets filled, I imagined, with whistles, compasses, pencils, pencil sharpeners and boxes of matches in case they got stranded in the wild bushland. There was a hunchbacked professor who seemed constantly to be looking at the floor. I hoped he wouldn't spot a rat. A snub-nosed middle-aged woman with elasticated stockings appeared to be his wife. The most unusual was a woman in her thirties, in a long denim skirt, a fleece jacket and spanking new, straight-out-of-the-box Adidas trainers. She walked straight up to me, as if about to make an arrest.

'I'm Elsie,' she said, 'and I have been told by my guru that I am the incarnation of the spirit of Effi Briest.' She spoke extremely fast as if she had to transmit the information before she blew up.

'That's nice,' I said. 'Liver and onions?'

After some wine had been opened, and downed, Harry and I felt we could leave the group in its own conversational fog.

'I think that Elsie is mad,' I told Harry.

'Believe me,' he said, 'I've been listening to them; they're all clinically insane. But what did you expect – did you think that any English people in their right minds would want to follow in the footsteps of a fictional heroine?'

'That's the business model of the Schloss, isn't it? To bring mad people together over the Internet and then entertain them in the real world.'

'At least they're not demanding a Schloss with ghosts,' said Harry.

And yet after we had pushed them all upstairs to bed, I began to wonder if the Schloss was not, after all, haunted. Just as I was beginning an email to Lena I heard a long penetrating female scream followed by a crash. It was, I suspected, the professor's wife and could only imagine what he was doing to her. Then came a manly shout, and a crash. And yet another desperate cry.

'What the hell's happening?' Joined by Harry – a little unsteady on his feet because, as he said, he had been consulting 'Dr Johnnie Walker' – and Lutz, I galloped up the stairs. We were confronted with guests rubbing their backs and visibly upset.

'Bed collapsed,' said one of the fishermen-vested guests who, I was happy to see, had changed into striped flannel pyjamas. 'Thought it was an earthquake. Was just about to take a tent outside when I heard everyone else.'

Lutz went into his room and slid under the rubble of the IKEA bed. He called me over.

'Someone's been loosening the screws,' he said. 'It must be sabotage.'

chapter 10

The Food of Empire

Outside a wind howled from the east. 'It's a sign that spring is about to begin,' said Lutz, 'every sailor knows that.' Lutz was talking a lot, perhaps because he wanted to deflect blame for the collapsing beds. As far as the Fontane-fans were concerned, he need not have bothered. They were yawning but, after Darren had poured coffee down their throats, they were happily getting into padded anoraks, ready for the tour.

Harry had worked out a route that combined Fontane sites with nearby pubs. I decided to come along too in case someone sober was needed to drive back the minibus. We bumped the bus over the driveway – now full of potholes eaten into the road by the months of snow – and set out for a place called Hankels Ablage, the Hankel warehouse.

'That's where the aristo officer Botho von somebody-or-other meets his lover in...'

'*Irrungen und Wirrungen*,' I inserted, naming the Fontane book (*Errors and Confusions*). Thinking: there could be no better way of describing my botched attempt to set up in the German countryside.

'That's it. They'll love it; it's romantic and, according to the Internet, there's a pub nearby. To warm up.'

We glanced at our passengers. I expected them to be nodding off, but they all seemed alert in a glassy-eyed kind of way, staring out of the window. We had apologised to them for their night-time interruption and they seemed to have accepted the incident as a curious fact – perhaps they now thought that all East German beds were structurally unstable – without demanding an explanation or threatening to sue. So far so good: but the mystery remained.

'Do you think Lutz cocked up?' I asked Harry.

'Nah,' he said, his face flickering briefly with irritation when the instructions on the GPS directed him down a muddy lane. 'Someone did it.'

'Lutz thinks Uwe did it.'

'Well, he would, wouldn't he? But what does Sherlock Holmes say: you need motive and opportunity for a crime. Where's the motive with Uwe? Frankly, I'm not so sure about Lutz. He went a bit crazy on those rats. Uwe doesn't work in a circus – how was he supposed to get a family of rats and smuggle them into the attic?'

'Lutz is my rock,' I said, ending the discussion.

I pondered the problem for a while as we approached the town of Zeuthen.

'Do you think it could have been mad Elsie? Hers was the only bed not to fall down.'

Harry looked at her in the rear-view mirror. She had her make-up compact open to check her lipstick wasn't smudged – or maybe to study us.

'Why would she do something like that?' whispered Harry, making a show of turning on the radio to confuse any of the eavesdropping passengers.

'Mad is mad,' I said, 'you don't need a motive.'

'I'll keep an eye on her,' said Harry and parked with a flourish at Hankels Ablage, next to the brown, sludgy Dahme river, as romantic as sewage works. The history of the place was simple enough to explain: the Hankel family had bought the place to store timber in the year of the French Revolution, then over the years it became a stop on the local railway. The family built a boarding house there and Fontane decided to set there the culmination of a love affair, the doomed misalliance between a weak aristocrat and a strong working woman. Harry explained this to the passengers in a hurried way to disguise his lack of facts. I had a small guidebook with me and I resolved that once we got into the building, I would give the Fonty-groupies a better picture. We ran through the screeching wind, from the minibus to the Fontane exhibition. 'At least it's not snowing, just a bit of rain,' called out the hunchbacked professor, and I marvelled yet again at the energy invested by English people in pointless conversation about the weather. 'Yes,' shouted back his wife, 'it's so fresh, isn't it?'

Once inside the hardy travellers shook off the rain like Labradors after taking a dip in the sea. Apart from a few photographs of Fonty, and the warehouse as it once was, there was nothing to look at, so I cleared my throat, and half-read from the guide book.

'As you will recall, Baron Botho von Rienäcker meets the tailor Magdalene Nimptsch during a boating party. She lives with her adoptive mum in a cottage near Berlin Zoo; he comes from an aristocratic family that is running out of money...'

My little audience was rapt. Only Harry was fidgeting, having noticed that the Anlage no longer served beer. Mad Elsie also seemed absent, staring out of the window at the rain.

'They meet here at the Ablage, but suddenly three army friends of Baron Botho arrive with their mistresses and he realises that Magdalene – who is called Lene throughout the work – can never be his wife, because she comes from a different world.' Lene, I thought: Lena. Where are you?

'Botho marries his rich cousin but doesn't love her. Lene,' I cleared my throat and hoped my Fonty-fans did not notice that I was taking this personally, 'Lene is smarter than her lover, always knew it wouldn't work and marries an older man, Gideon Franke. Lene explains that she isn't a virgin, Gideon isn't bothered – he has spent time in America so in Fonty's eyes is a man of the world – but goes to Botho to find out more. Botho understands that he has lost the love of his life because of a failure of courage, and that's about it.'

There was a silence, except for Harry's nervous fingers tom-tomming on the table in the cramped exhibition room.

'That's it? That's how it ends?' asked one of the vested men who had clearly not read the book.

'More or less. The Baron realises he's been an idiot when Gideon and Lena, sorry Lene, announce their marriage. He says "Gideon ist besser als Botho."'

'But Botho is richer,' said the professor, 'and has saved his estate.'

'And unhappy,' said the professor's wife, throwing him a sharp glance.

'What's this got to do with *Effi Briest*?' asked mad Elsie.

'Nothing,' I said. 'Different book.' I was too busy chewing on the question of Lena-Lene to be polite. Where was Lena now? How could I reconcile her with her own house?

'Life's hard, that's the connection. Fontane writes to his boss at the *Vossische-Zeitung*' – I flicked to the relevant page of the guidebook – 'the rules of life must apply, but they are hard.' I could feel my throat grow dry and stopped reading.

Harry spotted the warning sign and got to his feet.

'Right,' he said, 'time for a drink in the local pub and then off we go to Briest-land.'

And sure enough, Harry, who had the nose of a gun dog for locally brewed beer, found a pub that was a short drive away. It had plastic flowers on the wipe-clean 1980s Formica tables and was about as authentic as a mobile phone shop.

'It's built on the foundations of an original nineteenth-century warehouse,' improvised Harry. 'Fontane would have admired it, that's for sure. And he would have wished in his heart of hearts that the place would one day become a pub serving König Pilsener.'

'You're making a great author seem like a great alcoholic!' said the professor with an irritated buzz like a wasp trapped in a glass.

'Just a great talent, sir,' said Harry, with mocking respect, 'whose creative brain needed regular oiling.'

'Let's drink to creative oiling,' said fishermen's vest number one, who had in fact unzipped it to reveal a thick blue jumper of the sort worn by submarine officers.

'To creativity!' said the professor's wife.

'To oiling!' said Harry.

After Harry had knocked back three more glasses of in-a-gulp toasting, it became clear to me that I would have to do the next lap of driving. So while the group bonded with Harry, I spread out the map and tried to work out if we could get to Neuruppin – Fonty's birthplace – and back to our Schloss in time for a late lunch. It was difficult to concentrate; Lena's absence and Harry's presence befuddled the senses.

'What's your favourite book?' Mad Elsie was asking Harry. She was sitting next to him at the table, the professor's wife on the other side.

'*Effi Briest*, of course,' he said, though to my certain knowledge he had not read a single work by Fontane and was, truth be told, a Dan Brown man.

'It's perfect,' said Elsie, twirling her tangled blonde hair with her fingers.

'Well,' said Harry, 'it has only one flaw, really, doesn't it: the complete absence, somewhere in the middle, of a thirty-page sex scene.'

The assembled Fontane enthusiasts looked down at their beer without comment. It was all right to talk about the passion of Effi apparently, but not to talk of sweating bodies. Harry had committed blasphemy against the Master.

'Right,' I said, 'time to move!'

By the time that we had paid tribute to Fontane's birthplace – including several more Harry-led alcoholic toasts to the memory of the writer, and to his inspiration Walter Scott, and to his happy days as a correspondent in Britain – I could have poured the pilgrims out of the minibus. Britain was bonding with Germany, exactly as we had promised the embassy mandarins. With East Germany. True, alcohol was playing a role. But the shine in their eyes as they saw the statue of the writer in Neuruppin – that was our work! The professor was so drunk that he almost walked upright. 'Go and show it!' he shouted in broken German as we opened the front door. The quotation, of course, was from Fontane, who had seen a castle on an island in Scotland's Loch Leven which had reminded him of Schloss Rheinsberg or, as Harry had mischievously suggested, our very own Schloss. The sight had persuaded Fonty to embark on his wanderings in Brandenburg in search of countryside that was of a beauty equal, or superior, to what he had seen in Scotland. That story repeated to the Fonty-fans had provided an excuse to switch from beer to Scotch.

We were greeted not (as I had irrationally hoped) by Lena, returned from her self-imposed exile, but by the smell, no the aroma, of chicken and garlic. The wet literary enthusiasts gathered around the kitchen watching Darren put the finishing touches to his Trinidad stewed chicken; the oven spattered by oil, some chopped onion strewn on the floor, he had made a battlefield out of his workplace. But it was warm, and sweet – Darren had added brown sugar to the oil – and was not so sharp that it would send our guests running to put to the test our erratic plumbing. We all sat round the table slurping the food and although Darren smelled suspiciously of cannabis nobody complained. Lutz drew up a chair and whispered to me: 'I've fixed all the beds – they would survive a tsunami.' Mad Elsie was telling Harry that he reminded her of Major Crampas. She kept reaching across him for the bottle of Worcestershire sauce. Otherwise we all ate wordlessly, yet noisily, like pigs at a trough.

'So this is British food too?' asked Lutz.

'British food is the food of empire,' said the professor. Harry, fearing that we were going to be treated to a lecture, refilled the man's glass with some Chateau Aldi. The good stuff he had reserved for us. 'Apart from the breakfast bacon and things like Yorkshire pudding and fish and chips, we stole a lot of our recipes. There's nothing more British than chicken masala, which is now the country's favourite dish. Yet we stole it from the Indians and made it our own.'

Harry sighed loudly and plonked the whole bottle in front of the professor, hoping, presumably, to send him into a deep sleep mid-sentence. Somehow, in doing so, he managed to brush against Mad Elsie who was glowing, presumably with fresh air and booze, and who suddenly didn't look particularly mad at all.

Slopping liquid on the table, dropping rice – the boy would have to be taught manners – Darren refilled the plates.

'In Trinidad, the whole family cooks. My Dad cooked as well as my mom, he even taught her some recipes. It's not like here where if a man cooks well, he's like, gay.'

Lutz pushed his empty plate away from him.

'That's not true. In Germany some of our most manly men are cooks.'

'Yeah, well, whatever,' said Darren. 'Point is, even if we're just cooking for like three people, in our heads we're cooking for our family, like uncles and grandmothers and brothers and stuff. It's a celebration and even if the relatives are far away on the island, and we're in London, it doesn't matter because we've got them altogether in our heads. So we don't make it too sweet, because Uncle Fred, he's got sugar-disease, can't eat sugar, and not too chewy, because old granddad's lost his teeth.'

It was the longest speech I had heard from Darren and it reminded me that he really did care about cooking. I was sure now that Darren's passion for cooking had disturbed Lena, displaced her. Whoever controlled the stove controlled the heart, the whole rhythm of the place. This was more than getting a teenager in to fry up a few eggs, it was about controlling territory. Maybe she thought Harry and I had pushed Darren into the kitchen, in order to drive her out? I would have to find a way to reassure her. Left to his own devices, Darren would expand and expand, making us all honorary members of his Caribbean family. Soon we would all be playing in a steel band and limbo-dancing.

When the dishes were cleaned, the Fontane brigade was sent upstairs for a siesta. I sat down with Lutz and Darren to discuss the bed-crash. Harry had disappeared upstairs a quarter of an hour earlier, mumbling something about urgent business.

'Lutz,' I said, a little nervously, 'are you absolutely sure that you put those beds together properly?'

He didn't take offence.

'Of course,' he said. 'I checked them again this morning when you were on tour. IKEA makes its beds so it's enough to loosen one screw – one single screw – to make everything fall apart. The trick is to know which is the master screw. When you put it together, you don't notice. But anyone who has worked in a furniture removal business knows the trick, they all know.'

'The black magic of IKEA,' I said, with some admiration. They had taken a cliché – the man's got a screw loose – and made a whole system out of it. Like most chaotic organisers, I am in awe of people with a system.

'What's all this about?' asked Harry, suddenly descending the staircase.

'Where have you been?' I asked.

'Elsie asked me to check her bed was safe to sleep on.'

'Aha.'

Lutz and Darren exchanged glances.

'And how did you do that?'

'Tested the mattress. Can't be too careful if there is a saboteur at large.'

'No,' I said, 'can't be too careful.'

Lutz developed his view that Uwe was the evil genius behind the destruction of the beds.

'And why would he do that?' Harry asked.

It was a legitimate question. But I could see some kind of pattern emerging. Perhaps Uwe wanted to wreak some kind of revenge on Lutz. After all, Lutz had all but called Uwe a liar about the provenance of the rats in the attic. It could be that Uwe had introduced the rats and wrecked the beds – but why would he do all that just to get back at Lutz?

'Maybe he's just a nasty kid,' said Lutz.

Darren had made some tea, Trinidad style, with rum and sugar. It was high time that Lena came back and stopped us drinking ourselves to death. Suddenly Darren remembered something.

'I saw something mighty strange in town yesterday when I was shopping.'

'Not shopping for marihuana, I hope, Darren,' said Harry. 'We had a little conversation about that, you may remember.'

'No, Uncle Harry. Just buying some paprika and bananas. I saw that Uwe going into the rat-house.'

'That'll be Rathaus,' said Lutz.

'That's what I said. He was shaking hands with this little guy in the foyer, old – your age, Uncle Harry, but kind of fitter – and then I saw the old man give him an envelope. It was cash, I was sure it was.'

'Can't be sure of that,' I said.

'The mayor and Uwe,' said Lutz, 'there's a connection.'

'Well, they are family,' I said, 'that's not a secret. It's why we hired Uwe in the first place.'

'So what was so strange about the meeting, Darren?'

'That Uwe kept laughing, Uncle Harry, and you know, he didn't seem to be the laughing kind.'

We agreed with Darren. Uwe was not a laugher. A plan was needed. Lutz was in favour of grabbing Uwe and water-boarding him until he told us the truth.

Harry agreed.

'Great British invention, water-boarding,' he said.

'American,' I said.

'Stasi,' said Lutz.

Which gave me an idea. Perhaps Harry could fish around in the Stasi Secret Police archives in Berlin to see if there was anything on the mayor. Harry agreed.

'We can always torture Uwe later,' he said.

At which point I left the table to sit next to the fire and refresh my memory on the rules of cricket.

The next day Harry took the Fontane-fans, including mad Elsie, who continued to make large spaniel eyes at him, to Caputh. Fonty had called the place the Chicago of Brandenburg. This had captured Harry's imagination. As a young man he had spent a summer working at the *Chicago Tribune* and learning the mechanics of 'hard-nosed hard news' while drinking with the red-nosed soft-brained crime reporters at the Matchbox bar on Milwaukee Avenue. Not that Caputh was exactly Al Capone-land but Fonty had been there, Albert Einstein had a summer cottage near the lake, and so, of course, there were pubs for tourists. The Harry model of literary tourism (sense of place + alcohol = empathy with writer) was going to be wheeled out for the second day running. As Harry climbed behind the wheel, I noticed that Elsie had claimed the front passenger seat.

I had decided to stay in Alt-Globnitz for the day. We needed to start putting together the local cricket team. The only practice pitch I could find was the rough grassland behind the old Soviet barracks, a twenty-five-minute walk out of town. It was a strange place.

The first impression was that the barracks had been abandoned the day before; windows were open, banging in the wind; the parade ground was empty but the adjoining garages were still heavy with the smell of spilt oil. There was a disused petrol station; warehouses with open gates; the creak of timber. The Russians had removed every fitting, every bit of electrical wire; anything that could be useful was taken back home. The ovens had been lifted out, leaving only a black patch. How many men had it taken to lever out the baking oven? Ten, twelve?

The grass matched the building; it had been chewed up years ago by T-72 tanks and had never recovered. There were clods of earth everywhere, molehills. Strategically placed piles of cow dung suggested at least that the field was safe to set foot on: no hidden Russian mines tucked under the soil.

It was cold again and the seven men in front of me were shivering like jelly. The more athletic were bouncing up and down; most concentrated on drawing warmth from their cigarettes. All looked depressed, under orders. We had our four workers without Uwe. They were still being paid even though we had excused them from work for the three days that the Fonty-fans were in residence. Today they were being paid for playing cricket and I guessed they would have preferred to be mixing cement at the house; at least there they would be given free helpings of Trinidad chicken stew. Horst meanwhile had roped in Bernie from his t'ai chi course, and who was helping out at the hairdresser's sweeping up hair, a so-called one-euro job. He looked a bit weedy but some of the world's best cricketers had looked underfed and run-down, so there was cause for hope. Peter the plumber had turned up, as had Reckless Robert, the Sparkasse boss. Horst had talked them into it at Gundi's the previous night and they both looked as if they regretted their decision. Still, Peter had made good money out of unblocking our toilets and could probably hope for more. Robert had given us a bridging loan and, like all sensible bank managers in these prudent times, needed to keep an eye on his investment. I had hoped to have Gundi along – she was after all more athletic, indeed more masculine than any of the others – but Horst had ruled this to be a break of village etiquette.

It was for the men, he said, to defend the honour of the country against whatever weak-kneed pigeon-chested team that could be fielded by the English. The fact that Gundi had strong traces of a moustache did not, he said firmly, make her a man and there was certainly no doubting Horst on this point. There was hope though that Gundi could force one of her ex-boyfriends, perhaps Knut the Wrestler, to join the side.

Horst and I took stock of the 'team', and I remembered the Duke of Wellington's words as he surveyed his ragamuffin British troops before going into battle with Napoleon: 'My God, they may not frighten the enemy but they as sure as hell scare me'. Between us lay a long black bag with some second-hand kit discovered in the British Embassy basement: two bats, some helmets, leg-pads and the stumps. 'Right,' I said with a show of confidence, 'Stumps!' I held them up. Then I stuck them into the rock-hard ground. This was so difficult that I had to take my shoe off and use it as mallet. There was a risk, I could see, of appearing ridiculous. But no one sniggered as I placed the bails delicately on the stumps.

'Now,' I said, 'a man has to stand in front of the stumps and defend them. With his bat. Block the ball...' I demonstrated what I thought was a graceful forward movement. Something clicked in my back but I ignored it: this was no time to display weakness. '... or whack it hard.' I made a show of smashing an imaginary ball for six.

'If the bowler, or anyone else for that matter, knocks the bails off the stumps, the batsman is out.'

'Dead,' chipped in Horst.

'Off the field,' I said.

'How do you win?' That from Reckless Robert the banker. I still hadn't ruled out the possibility of unlocking funds from him, so I was particularly patient.

'Good question. The batsman knocks the ball, then runs to the other wicket and exchanges position with the second batsman. That's a run.'

'Like... a run on the bank?' asked Robert, dully. I could see this was going to be difficult.

'No, it's a point. Lots of runs mean lots of points.'

It was quite simple, I explained. One team tried to destroy another according to a set of obscure rules. It was war; it was life. And because the British had invented it, it was said to be the very essence of fair play.

'But don't players take bribes?' asked one of the house builders. 'I read somewhere...'

'Don't believe everything you read!' I snapped.

'And what about drugs?' This from Feckless Bernie, the barbershop boy...

'They don't help.' The game was so slow and aimless that most of the spectators already thought they were on LSD.

I looked up into their baffled faces; it was as if I had given them a text by Hegel to study and memorise. Horst caught my gaze and wandered to his Passat Estate, returning with a blackboard. The chalk screeched as he drew the positions.

'That's it,' I said, pointing to the blackboard, 'one team has all eleven players on the pitch. There is the bowler who throws the ball, the wicketkeeper who crouches behind the batsman waiting for him to make a mistake and nine others spread around waiting to catch the ball. The other team has only two players on the pitch at any one time. Two batsmen.'

'What do the others do?' asked Robert from the Sparkasse.

'They sit on the sidelines, drink beer, crack jokes and wait for their turn.'

There was a rumble of approval from the men.

'You will also notice,' I said, 'that no one has to run very far. It is therefore the perfect game for someone not in the first flush of youth. Now who wants to try?'

There was an awkward shifting from foot to foot, as if I had asked the class to solve a difficult trigonometry problem.

Horst took over.

'Who here ever did civil defence studies at school?' He did not wait for an answer. 'Peter and Robert, obviously. Come up here.' The others had all been born after the fall of communism and had therefore been spared East German military training.

'Peter, you learned to throw a grenade, I think.'

Stroking his beer stomach, Peter acknowledged this was the case.

Horst handed him a leather ball and pointed to the wicket.

'There is the class enemy,' barked Horst, probably hoping to stir some long-dormant killer instinct from the plumber. The 'class enemy' – that was the all-purpose East German term for top-hatted capitalists and evil NATO generals.

'Now destroy!'

Peter took a short, puffing run, stretched back the arm carrying the ball and hurled it at the wicket.

It missed by at least three metres.

'So that's how capitalism triumphed over communism,' I said.

'Should have put on my glasses,' mumbled Peter.

Peter's failure, however, encouraged the rest of the team. It was definitely more satisfactory to throw a fantasy grenade than a real cricket ball.

I could see the determined look on their faces as they imagined the three pieces of wood to be their current enemy: an awkward boss, perhaps, or a critical wife. And it did not take much to explain that the throwing action of a grenade was essentially that of a cricket ball. In essence, it was just another form of skittles; bowling without the brains.

'Right,' said Horst, after about twenty minutes of pseudo-grenade throwing, 'now we need a batsman. Bernie!'

All my workers giggled and I knew why. Bernie had been jailed for three months for threatening to hit a foreigner – in fact a very suntanned German from Stuttgart – with a baseball bat. The young man might have looked a bit weedy but he certainly knew what to do with a bat.

'Right Bernie, take the bat, try to concentrate on hitting balls rather than humans and go to guard that wicket.' Bernie swaggered proudly toward the wooden stakes.

'Now Peter,' said Horst, 'I want you to throw your grenade at Bernie. Or rather at the stumps behind Bernie.'

Peter touched the ball with his mouth. 'Why's he doing that?' I asked Horst.

'He's taking the detonation pin out of the grenade in his imagination.'

Then he trundled up and tossed the cork-and-leather ball. Bernie had three seconds to react and chose to throw himself on the floor and clutch his head. The ball knocked down the stakes and Peter shouted 'Jaaaaa!' Robert clapped in solidarity with his contemporary, and a couple of my workers punched the air. Nobody much liked Bernie and it was very satisfactory to see him lying on a cowpat.

'This is a shit game,' he said in a muffled voice.

'You have to use your bat, Bernie,' I said. 'It takes courage to face up to a fast hard ball that is coming towards you with the force of a Ferrari.' Actually Peter's delivery was more the speed of a Trabant in winter.

'But what if it hits me?' whispered Bernie, picking himself up.

'The batsman has a choice: either to hit the ball with all his strength or to kill it, to stop it gently with the bat so that it can't be caught by anybody.'

'It's hit or kill?' asked Bernie, showing interest for the first time.

'The ball, yes,' I said, 'We don't do this to humans.' I reminded myself to check all bats were put back in the bag after the end of our practice session.

We trained for another thirty minutes, until the boys started to complain that it was too cold to catch balls, and we headed back to our cars. I overheard two of them analysing cricket:

'Only the British could dream up a game of hitting grenades.'

'Crazy people.'

Chapter 11

An Inspector Calls

It was the last night for the Fontane fans and after a couple of days of Harry's energetic tour guidance they were exhausted. Darren had offered to make a more traditional British dish – sausages and mash – but the Fonty gang was determined to have Trinidad stewed chicken again.

'We could do something German,' I proposed. 'Potato soup? Meatballs in caper sauce?'

'No, thanks,' said fishermen's vest number one. 'We need Darren's rice to soak up the booze that Harry has been infusing into us.'

Lena or no Lena, there was a kind of warmth to the Schloss that evening. The group had bonded and learnt a little. It was pretty lonely to be a British admirer of nineteenth-century German literature. As for Harry and me, we were just relieved that we hadn't lost or killed any of them. It augured well for the Schloss. Elsie was making plans for Harry to come and visit her in Bournemouth but Harry said nothing or rather just contrived to feed everybody his extravagant myths.

'Did you know that they've named a bar after me in Venice?' he asked Elsie.

'Harry's Bar?' said Elsie, wide-eyed.

'Nonsense,' interrupted the professor, 'it's named after an alcoholic American student who bankrolled Cipriani.'

'Oh, not that Harry's Bar,' said Harry, 'mine is altogether more interesting, just off the Calle Vallaresso.' He then launched into a long implausible speech about how he had won a large amount of money at poker and had been persuaded to invest in 'liquid assets' – a bar specialising in rum cocktails – how he had been cheated out of his cash but how, finally, in some arrangement that involved meeting men in dark glasses and panama hats, they had agreed to keep his name on the front of the building.

Stories just seemed to roll out of Harry like a grand unfurling Icelandic saga and the narrative flow was matched by the flow of wine. To keep costs down we had poured supermarket wine into carafes for the English visitors and kept back the good stuff for ourselves. There was no sense in wasting it on visitors who, by the looks of things, were about to fall into a deep happy sleep. They were due to be taken to the airport at 10 a.m. – Uwe had been round to the house to confirm that he would drive them to Schönefeld – and could sleep relatively long in the morning. Even so, we had to prop them up as they ascended the stairs.

'There will be Alka-Seltzer on the menu tomorrow morning,' I told Darren as I returned to the salon. Darren finished washing the kitchen – though in such a slipshod way that I knew I would have to do it a second time – and went to his room. Harry had got him a portable television so that he wouldn't be tempted to sample the nightlife of Alt-Globnitz and get into trouble. Sometimes at night I would pass his room and hear the clamour of Sat 1 – a little sex, a little violence, the usual mixed grill – and wonder whether he was happy. A teenage boy needed friends if only to boast and swagger, an audience. The Schloss may have been a useful refuge for him, far away from the curious gaze of the police, but I didn't want it to become a prison.

Harry and I got out the chessboard and played a few rounds of Blitzchess – moves had to be made within ten seconds. It was a caricature of the game, we played for money and Harry always won, but I preferred it to the more reflective version. Harry would have used the long pauses contemplating moves to talk about Lena and, in truth, I didn't want to talk about her. I was about to lose another ten euros on a game when I heard a noise from upstairs: a rapid pitter-patter of feet from one of the bedrooms to one of the bathrooms. And again: another person on the trot. And the sound of a man trying to vomit.

'Make your move,' said Harry.

'Can't you hear something?'

'Just someone going to the toilet,' said Harry. 'Happens around the world all the time.'

I stood up and Harry reluctantly joined me.

Upstairs, the Schloss had become Dante's Inferno. Elsie, pale as paper, was trying to support herself on the wall moving unsteadily, step by step, down the corridor. One of the pyjama-ed fishermen's vesters was holding his mouth, waiting for the toilet where someone else was making vomiting sounds. The professor's wife had tipped out a cactus so that her husband could retch into the pot. Half an hour earlier the whole corridor had been in deep hibernation; now they had been brought back to life in the most radical way.

The acid odour of fresh vomit; that special noise, like that of a shovel scraping snow, associated with dry retching.

'It's food poisoning,' I told Harry. 'Get Darren up.'

Harry was helping Elsie to sit, rather than fall, on the floor.

'My head's spinning,' she croaked, 'I've got to lie down.' She hunched into a tiny blonde ball in the corridor.

I went to get a bowl of hot water, some towels and a few plastic bags for those who weren't able to get into the bathrooms. By the time I came back, Darren was on his feet.

'It wasn't me, Uncle Harry, honest!' pleaded Darren. I could see that Harry was only a short step away from slapping his nephew. 'You're not ill, are you?' Neither of you is ill! So it can't be the food.'

I was not very sure of Darren's logic. It could be that some of the chicken was rotten and some not. But we had helped ourselves from the same pot.

'Maybe it was stomach flu,' I said doubtfully.

'But it's hit them all at almost exactly the same time,' said Harry, 'what kind of flu does that?'

Darren was looking scared. He had been in some scrapes in his short life – carjacking had been particularly good fun – but he could see the German cops accusing him of attempted murder.

'I'm telling you the food was fine. I tasted it myself and nothing happened to me.'

I decided to ring Lena. OK, perhaps she would not answer again – if she didn't, I would use Harry's phone, she wouldn't ignore that – and she was probably still pissed off with me, but she would understand what was going on. She knew about food, knew about kitchens. I needed her advice.

She picked up the phone and though there was an edge to her voice I felt a surge of relief.

'Thank God,' I said, 'Hi.'

'Hi.'

'Where are you?' I asked.

'At Adele's.' A psychotherapist friend; not a good augury.

I explained the situation to her and I could hear that she was shocked. Still, she was calm and precise, more Hamburg than Sorrento, and I was grateful for that.

'Give me Darren,' she said.

We put the phone on loudspeaker.

'Tell me exactly what you put into that stew,' she told Darren.

'Sure,' said Darren, his voice shaking a bit, 'where do I begin?'

'At the beginning.'

'Well, first I made the green seasoning, threw chives and thyme and pepper and stuff into the blender. Then put it into the fridge.

'You had chicken stew, the day before?' Lena was well informed. Had she been talking to Lutz in my absence?

'Yeah.'

'Did you mix the old green sauce with the new green sauce?'

'No, ma'am.' The phone was on loudspeaker and both Harry and I caught Lena's sigh on the other end. We both recognised it as an expression of deep scepticism.

'Darren, tell me about the chicken.'

'I just seasoned it, put on salt and pepper and left it to marinade in the fridge.'

'Was there any other raw meat in the fridge?'

'No, for sure not.'

'Where did you get the chicken? Did you use some of ours?'

'No, the boss' – Darren looked over at me, I was the boss – 'told me the hens in the back are kept for eggs. I got the chicks in the supermarket. Good price. Real good.'

Harry and I glanced at each other. It took a lot to persuade the Alt-Globnitz supermarket to discount its prices.

'And then?'

'I heated the oil.'

'Fresh?'

'Sure, put in dark sugar, garlic, waited for the sauce to change colour, go real dark, then added the chicken, turned them a bit...'

'The chicken was done? Was it red in the middle?'

'Put in a fork, ma'am, it was done.'

Lena pushed hard, like a *Tatort* detective wanting to get the crime solved before the beginning of Anne Will. The direct suspect, as far as I could see, was the chicken. It could be that Darren was a secret stickler for hygiene but if he hadn't cleaned the knives properly, chopped up a dubious chicken and then chopped up something else and even forgot to wash his hands, then we might have cracked the case.

'And the rice?'

'Freshly made.' This was true; I remembered seeing it bubbling and steaming in the corner of the kitchen.

'Did you leave the pot unattended?'

'No, ma'am, I was watching it the whole time.'

Lena asked for me.

'What do you think?' she asked.

'Don't know. Could be that we're not amazingly precise with our hygiene compliance. And chickens are tricky – it's that camp-actor bug.'

'Campylobacter.'

'Whatever. But what bothers me is that neither Harry nor Darren nor I have got anything. It just hit the guests. And they're not behaving the way I did when I got sushi-poisoning.'

'You mean when you projectile-vomited on the Japanese Ambassador?' I could hear a hint of a chuckle, of a shared warm memory in her voice. How strange that we were making up our quarrel amid scenes of Goya-esque horror. But I was right: they were reacting differently. The professor in particular was swaying as if he were seasick; that is, it seemed to be his sense of balance that was affected, and that in turn was making him nauseous. Everybody wanted to be sick but as far as I could see not much was coming up. 'They've got the runs,' said Harry, 'and they're a bit feverish. But really serious puking, well, it's no worse than an average London pub on a Friday night.'

'Something's not quite right,' said Lena. 'If Darren's telling us the truth, his food was OK. I'll come down in the morning. In the meantime make sure they get plenty of water to drink.'

'Sure,' I said. 'Lena?'

'Yes?'

'Why did you storm off like that?'

'I needed to think.'

Why did women say that so often? Why did they run away to think, like they had just robbed a bank? Why couldn't they just lie on the sofa, watch a soap – and think? Did the proximity of men stop them thinking, confuse their thoughts?

'All right,' I said, 'I suppose. Just come back, we need you here.'

'It certainly sounds like you're all making a complete mess without me.' The phone went dead.

It was two o'clock in the morning and the patients had calmed down; their fever had ebbed and almost everybody had slipped into a fitful slumber. One of the fishermen's vest guests had moved his mattress off his bed and placed it near the bathroom, so sure was he that the trouble would return. The corridor resembled an army field hospital: bowls outside the rooms, soiled clothes, plastic water bottles.

'They can't fly in the morning,' said Harry.

'I'll change the flights,' I said, reaching for the laptop and thinking: this is going to be a financial disaster.

Darren, his hard-guy image forgotten, seemed to be on the brink of tears. He wandered around downstairs, staring blankly at the kitchen surfaces as if trying to identify some food bacteria with his naked eye. I did not blame him: he had cooked for his family for years in a far grubbier environment and nothing had ever happened. On the contrary, cooking was the one thing in his life that he had ever been praised for; it was his one publicly acknowledged talent.

'Sit down with us,' I told him. Harry looked thoughtful, biting his nails. I needed a cigarette but decided to hold off; I did not want the place to smell like a nineteenth-century gin palace when Lena came back.

'Right, Darren,' said his uncle, 'we're going to give you the benefit of the doubt. If it wasn't your cooking, what was it? Could someone have put something into the stew?'

Darren shook his head. 'That guy Uwe was here for a bit but before I had begun the cooking.' He thought a bit harder. 'Lutz was hanging around too, fixing something but he knocked off early.'

It was true Lutz had left unusually early; had said he wanted to celebrate his wedding anniversary although he didn't actually say whether he was going to do this with his wife.

'Nothing else?'

'Nah, it was a bit boring. You were out, Uncle, with the guests, and you,' he said with a nod in my direction, 'were doing cricket training.'

'So,' mused Harry, 'either Uwe or Lutz could have done something. But we don't know what. And we don't know why. That's not a great start. What do you reckon, Hercule Poirot?'

'Well, there could be a completely different explanation, I suppose. Some strange bug caught in the Mark.'

'To which I'm immune,' said Harry.

'On the other hand, there's a pattern. The rats, the collapsing beds, now this – it could be sabotage.'

'By Uwe, you mean,' said Harry. 'But there is a problem, it's only Lutz making the connection. I never really bought Lutz's claim that Uwe had placed rats onto the attic to screw up the Schloss. Have you ever tried to smuggle rats anywhere? How the hell do you do it?'

Harry was getting into his stride now.

'As for the beds falling apart, we've only got Lutz's word about the loose screw. Maybe he just put them together badly. Or maybe he's playing some kind of game.'

'Like what?' I couldn't credit Lutz with trying to wreck the Schloss. There were a dozen ways that he could have prevented Lena and me from purchasing the house. But he hadn't. He seemed genuinely happy that we had taken it over.

Neither Harry nor I could figure out what to do about this information. Darren was not exactly an impeccable source at the moment.

'OK, this is what I propose,' said Harry. 'Tomorrow we follow Lutz, and next day we follow Uwe. Discreetly like the bloke from the Raymond Chandler books.'

'Philip Marlowe.'

'That's it. We give Lutz the day off – in fact we give everyone the day off. Uwe too, don't want him creeping around – and just keep an eye on him.'

'What will that bring?'

'Don't know. More information than we have now. We're stuck in this bloody house and we don't have a clue what's happening around us. If someone wants to put you out of business we've got to dig a bit.'

'That's cool, Uncle,' said Darren. 'I could tail Lutz around.'

'You don't think you might stick out a bit?' said Harry, patting his nephew's shoulder. 'We could only use you at night.'

'Because, you know, young people have better eyesight,' I hurried to add in case Darren got the wrong impression.

'And now bed,' said Harry 'I want to get to the bottom of this as soon as we can.' I went outside for my cigarette and knew I wouldn't be able to sleep.

Darren was up before anyone else the next morning.

'Hot tea is the thing,' said Darren, 'that's what my family does.'

'Happens a lot in your family, does it?' I asked.

'No, never, but we know what to do.'

'Just in case.'

'Yeah, just in case. Tea with a dash of ginger. No milk, no sugar.'

'Sounds good,' I said, 'but let me take the cups to the patients, OK? I don't want you being crucified.'

'Stoned, more like it,' said Harry, who had just skipped downstairs as if he had woken up from a long satisfying slumber in the Alps, stirred only by the distant tinkle of goat bells and yodelling peasants.

He gave his nephew a friendly clip around the ear, advised him to take a shower and together we transported the trays of ginger tea to the convalescent Fonty-fans.

'My stomach still hurts,' complained Elsie.

'At least you don't look green anymore,' said Harry, handing her a cup. 'Drink this and soon you'll be back on your feet.' She was, in fact, already on her feet and was drifting along the corridor like Ophelia. Naturally Elsie saw herself in a different role.

'Oh Harry,' she said, 'I thought I was going to die last night, just like Effi. Wouldn't that have been romantic, to have passed away in the very same house that she stayed?'

I threw Harry an inquisitive look. He seemed to have rather embellished the Schloss's contribution to German literature. But he carried on distributing tea to the needy – to the professor, who this morning had the pallor and astonishing red lips of a vampire, to his long-suffering wife who was packing her clothes for departure. As I suspected, she was a Littlewoods mail-order shopper: her bag was filling up with floral-print dresses that had looked good on the pages of the catalogue and which she had no doubt expected to wear to a string of interesting cocktail parties with Fontane scholars. We hadn't quite come up to scratch. I knew that we had let them down. It was all very well to keep the visitors on an alcoholic high throughout the trip, in a kind of blissful oblivion, but when their stomachs curdled, the Harry school of tourism looked a little like confidence trickery. So for now we were concentrating on damage limitation: keep their metabolism stable enough so that they were still registering a pulse and then dispatch them to Britain before they could sue us. Even the suspicion of food poisoning would put the Schloss out of business.

Apart from Elsie in her almost transparent nightdress, everyone was wearing towelled dressing gowns as if they had packed for a visit to a spa with mud pack treatment.

'It's as if we've all been invited to the Playboy Mansion, don't you think, professor,' said Harry, 'with you playing the Hugh Hefner role of course.' The professor was too physically drained to protest. The priority, I decided, was to clean up the place as quickly as possible and free it from the clammy memory of sickness.

But before I could get everybody organised for a Blitz-clean, a key rattled in the door and Lena appeared.

'Hi!' I shouted from upstairs, turning away from the patients.

'Hello!' echoed Harry.

Darren, pottering in the kitchen, nodded shyly.

'This is the woman who was going to take you all on an *Effi Briest* ride across the fields,' Harry told the guests. 'Looks like we'll have to just stick to an ambulance ride.'

Lena put down her case and threw off her goose-down coat.

'Smells like a zoo in here,' she said.

'It's my new aftershave, Animal Magic,' I replied, coming down the stairs to kiss her. She accepted a peck on the cheek.

I waited while her gaze lasered through the salon. In truth, it looked pretty much as it did when she angrily evacuated the place. The only problem was the upstairs chaos.

'Why don't you put your coat on again and we'll go for a walk,' I proposed, signalling to Harry that he and Darren should start cleaning upstairs. With any luck by the time we got back the guests would be out of their dressing gowns. 'We need to have a chat, don't we?'

Actually, it was Lena who had to talk. She had, after all, been closeted away in Berlin for days, stoking her anger and frustration. My job was to listen, I knew that. And yet I had always found it difficult to concentrate when being reprimanded. It was no different at school when my Latin teacher would complain about a piece of bad homework. I would look down at the floor and count the numbers of cracks in the wood. Or pretend to look him in the eyes but actually stare over his shoulder and watch the birds through the window. Every male, however mentally underdeveloped – even a Hollywood director – understands by now that he has to master the art of empathetic listening, that the ear is the vital male organ. It is just that it's so difficult in practice.

It started off reasonably enough. Lena was taking us back to our New Year's Eve dinner at Borchardt's. I remembered it well: Kobe steak.

'I admit I took you by surprise,' she said, 'I didn't want to turn your life upside down.'

'That's OK,' I said, 'I've lived my life upside down. You simply put me the right way up.'

'The fact is when I inherited the Schloss you were already fed up with journalism, right? You had got your sabbatical,' she said. 'It was not as if you actually gave up anything very much to come to Brandenburg.'

'Well, I turned my back on civilisation. I gave up intellectual conversation, going to the cinema, Kobe steak. It was not without sacrifices.'

Lena was already growing impatient.

'Listen to me now,' she said sternly. You could just go back to Berlin tomorrow and go back to writing about polar bears in Berlin zoo.'

'And Nazis.'

'Yes, yes. But my point is this: you don't have a stake in the Schloss. But I do – for me, it is life-changing. The idea that I can live in the same place as my ancestors, perhaps discover their ancient rhythms – that really matters. The Schloss is about me, about me finding me. Not some laddish game involving bacon and eggs and a lot of booze.'

I thought about this for a while. We were marching towards the café of Lutz's wife, Annaliese. It was a neutral place, where we could maybe sort out our differences. Lena was passionate about the Schloss. I knew that. Everyone knew that. Then why walk out on the project?

'We were just trying to find a way of financing the place.'

'It was more like a coup d'état,' she said.

'So that's a reason to run away? You're the boss, it's your place – why didn't you fight for it?'

'It stopped feeling like my place the moment that Darren took over the cooking.'

'We can change that. Actually we will have to.'

There were no other customers in the café. I took in the little plastic buckets on the tables – to dispose of breakfast debris, the used butter packets and mini milk containers – and shuddered a little.

Lena greeted Annaliese and ordered coffee and a chocolate croissant. I just fiddled with the paper napkins.

'I don't like what you said about me not having a stake in the Schloss,' I said at last. 'I've got a stake in you, haven't I? The Schloss wasn't just about you finding your roots – it was about making time for each other again. You've forgotten that. When I fight for the Schloss, I'm fighting for you.'

Lena picked crumbs from her jumper.

'That's the problem, you see: I can't see that you are fighting, not really. You're too busy having fun.'

Fun? In IKEA? Dealing with the workers and with rats and living in a building site?

She never did get to finish her coffee. Lutz's wife, flat-faced, charming, always busy, came to our table.

'You've got food poisoning at the Schloss?' I had told Lutz early that morning, wanting him out of the house.

'Could be,' I said, 'we're not certain.'

'The Rathaus knows,' she said. 'One of my customers said they're sending a health inspector this morning.'

'Shit,' I said.

'Shit,' Lena said.

We rushed back and found Darren unhappily vacuum-cleaning, most of the guests with clothes on and Harry chatting up Elsie.

'How are the two lovebirds?' Harry asked. Lena glared. I filled him in, not pausing for breath. We all grasped the significance of a food inspector: the end of any sensible business plan for the Schloss.

'I'm going to sort out the fridges,' said Lena, 'we have to separate raw from cooked meat and if possible chuck out anything that looks dubious. Darren,' she shouted to make herself heard over the drone of the vacuum cleaner, 'get rid of all the kitchen rubbish – now!'

Harry and I looked at each other.

'How do the toilets look?'

'Don't ask,' said Harry and immediately rang Peter the Plumber.

Together we briefed the guests. If the inspector posed them any questions they were to say that they had enjoyed a delicious meal and were in the peak of health. Elsie offered to apply some of her make-up to anyone who still looked a little under the weather. Only the professor rebelled.

'Surely you don't expect me to lie to a German official.'

'Just be economical with the truth, professor,' advised Harry. 'I find that usually works for me.'

'Or you could say that you found the Caribbean pepper sauce a little too hot for your sensitive stomach,' I suggested.

'Nonsense, I've got a stomach like cast iron!' said the professor.

'Didn't look like it last night,' said Harry.

The doorbell rang and we all went to our stations, like sailors on a U-boat preparing to dive. But it was only Peter the Plumber, faster off the mark than any plumber I have ever known; Harry must have promised him double rates in return for his discretion. Plumbers are in possession of more dirty secrets than confessional priests.

Peter had completed his messy task by the time the inspector came an hour later. I was pleased to see that he arrived on a motorbike – that is, without any kind of laboratory sampling equipment. He was a young man with an Elvis quiff and seemed pleasant enough; Health and Hygiene expert in a town with so few hotels and restaurants was a sinecure and I wondered what strings were pulled with the mayor to have him installed.

'Pleased to meet you,' said Lena, who had at last assumed the role of Lady of the Manor. 'How can we help you?'

'Health and Hygiene,' said the man. I saw him appraise Lena in a top-to-bottom look. Forget it, I wanted to tell him, keep your hands off her. 'We've had reports of a food poisoning outbreak.' He fumbled for a pen and a notebook.

'Village rumours, eh,' said Harry. 'Amazing what nonsense people talk when they're bored out of their minds. Nice bike.'

'Ride one yourself?' asked the inspector.

'Sure,' lied Harry, 'love it. We should get together sometime, have a few beers.'

'What have you got?'

'Er, nothing special.'

'A big bike?'

'Medium-ish. A, a, a BMW 500.'

'That's not big. You have problems on corners?'

'God, yes, corners sheer hell.'

I decided to intervene before Harry dug himself deeper into a hole.

'Would you like to meet our guests?' I asked, and, assuming the part of theatre impresario signalling Curtain Up, I waved to the tired group of Fonty enthusiasts. Elsie, I noticed, had indeed smothered fisherman's vest number two with pancake make-up. The effect was to make him look jaundiced.

'We had a really good meal,' said Elsie.

'Perhaps you would like some. I think we have some left over, don't we, Darren?'

The inspector politely declined. He was, after all, on duty. Lena opened the fridges.

'A bit cold to have all the windows open, isn't it?' asked the inspector. We wanted to expel the zoo-smell.

'You know how we British are, a hardy folk,' said Harry.

There are three kinds of German civil servant.
Type 1: hard-working, ambitious, unstable
Type 2: hard-working, blinkered
Type 3: lazy, but sharp-eyed
Our inspector was type 3.

'Is your stomach bothering you?' he asked Elsie in not-bad English, noting that she was rubbing her stomach. Harry threw her an anxious glance.

'Pregnant,' said Elsie. 'Not that it's any of your business.' She winked at Harry – as if to say 'just joking' – and I hoped that the inspector did not catch it.

'You look a strange colour,' said the official, registering fishermen's vest number two and the heavy coat of orange Clinique Bronzing Gel on his face. Fishermen's vest (he was wearing it again in preparation for the flight back to Britain) looked flustered but before he could reply, Darren – standing nearby– had sprung into action.

'You have a problem with me being black?' said Darren. 'Do you find black a strange colour?' The whole room watched as the inspector's eyes flickered with panic.

'I'm sure that the gentleman isn't racist, Darren,' said Lena. 'But I don't quite understand' – she said turning to the young official – 'why you are conducting a pseudo-medical examination? Surely you just want to know if the kitchen is clean and meets the hygiene standards.' She strode over to the oven.

Suddenly, the professor – obviously still weak – sat down at the table with a loud scraping of chair legs.

'And are you all right?' asked the inspector.

We held our breath.

'I'm fine, young man. And if I had more time I would be asking for a ride on your bike. I led the Oxford motorcycle safari across the Gobi Desert in 1969. I could show you a thing or two. But sadly,' and the professor did look a little sad, 'we have to leave for the airport soon.'

The inspector took the hint, asked Lena to sign a form, wished us well and drove off churning up ice and gravel. The professor high-fived Darren; we felt like resistance fighters in occupied Europe who had outwitted the enemy to live another day.

'Cool bike,' said Darren, staring enviously at the machine.

'Yes, cool bike, Darren,' said Harry. 'Now shut the bloody windows before we die of hypothermia. The smell of vomit never did anyone any harm. Right, Lena?'

Lena gave him a tight smile. Neither Harry nor I were out of the doghouse yet.

Chapter 12

Gargling with Scotch

After a long rainy night, the frogs went on the march. The male frogs had been croaking in the pond for a week, a ragged sing-song as raucous as fans on a football terrace. The females, hearing their potential mates, dropped what they were doing and without further ado started the trek to the pond. They were heavy with eggs and, though it was spring, there weren't that many insects to feed on. By the time they had fought their way across the fields they must have been exhausted and hungry. To avoid the necessity of carrying bottles of Evian like amphibian joggers, frogs simply sit in puddles and soak up water so they are not dehydrated by the time they have sex. But they have to be lucky to cross busy roads and come out alive on the other side. The mayor had not kept his end of the deal; I had hired locals to rebuild the Schloss, yet he had not planted a sign to alert drivers during the migration season. Lutz and I watched the frogs flopping and leaping, slaves to the sexual instinct, and wondered how to save them. So far they had been spared from slaughter under the wheels of a long-haul truck. Frankly, most trucks avoided Alt-Globnitz, preferring roads with burger-bars and Bulgarian prostitutes. It was only a matter of time, though, before a tractor produced tonnes of frog-mince.

'We need to erect our own warning sign,' said Lutz. He had been the first, in the early hours of the morning, to hear and understand the rustling noise, sense the movement. But I had not been as alert as I should have been, partly because I had not been talking much to Lutz. There had been a chill between us since I had spied on him.

After we had dispatched the Fontanistas back to Britain, Harry and I had gone in search of Lutz. He had the day off: what was he going to do, who was he going to meet? If he really was linked to the events in the Schloss, then surely he would be reporting to someone about the success or otherwise of the food-poisoning episode? It was an outside chance. On the other hand, he might just spend the day fixing his car. We were not tapping his phones or hacking into his email; we were merely trying to find out a bit more about a man whom we had automatically trusted. 'Just a bit of honest detective work,' said Harry, who had put on his trench coat, imagining that it made him look like a tough LA private eye, the kind of rugged anti-hero that put his shoes on the desk, gargled with Scotch and lit his cigarettes with matches scratched against his stubbled chin. In fact he looked more like Peter Sellers as Inspector Clouseau.

We reclaimed the Opel from Lena, and popped into Gundi's to find out if anyone had seen Lutz. Gundi shrugged, as if to say: He's an adult, he's male; he'll turn up. His wife at the café seemed to think that he was at the Schloss; we knew better. More by luck than by brilliant detection, we caught sight of him entering the Apotheke. It was already nearly closing time so we stood in the shadows waiting for him. After thirty minutes, Harry was growing impatient.

'What's he doing in there, re-inventing the bloody aspirin?'

I could tell from the switching on and off of lights exactly which rooms were being used. For at least two hours the lights were blazing in the bedroom of Doris Bonkerz's holiday apartment above the pharmacy where Lena and I had lived. Then there was darkness for an hour, no apparent movement. Good luck to Lutz, I thought, I just hope he keeps his socks on. Doris did not believe in superfluous heating. She wanted to save the planet even if it meant that her tenants froze to death. And he should be careful of the low-hanging light when he put his clothes back on again. Lutz eventually emerged from the front door after two hours.

'Well, that was a waste of time,' I said.

'No, it wasn't,' said Harry. 'Now we know he's having an affair with Doris Bonkerz.'

'Actually,' I reminded Harry, 'we don't even know that; all we know is that lights went on and lights went off. And even if he is having an affair with Doris, what does it matter? Nothing to do with us.'

'Of course it matters,' said Harry, his big manicured hands clenching and unclenching. 'He's passing on all the Schloss gossip to his fancy woman and who knows who she is talking to. We're going to have to watch Lutz very carefully.'

'Not tonight, please,' I said. 'I want to get back to Lena.'

We hadn't informed Lena about our undercover operations because she would have cut through its silliness, but also because she thought the world of Lutz. I did too, and my first instinct was to dismiss our spying mission as just another flawed Harry-inspired adventure. We had discovered absolutely nothing that would help us to work out why things were going wrong in the house. But Harry's moral outrage about what may or may not have been Lutz's dalliance with Doris started to colour my judgement too. It underlined the fact that we did not know much about the village: who was for us and who was against us. The following night we trailed Uwe – and discovered only that he went early to bed.

These outings gave me a bad conscience. What was I doing snooping on Lutz, by far and away my best mate in Alt-Globnitz? It was as if the Secret Police culture of the bad old days had somehow entered my bloodstream. As a result, I began to feel uneasy in Lutz's presence. We used to chat several times a day – over tea, over beer; mainly over beer. I had sorted out the technical problems of the renovation with him and we had conspired together to water down some of Lena's more extravagant plans. The Schloss looked the better for it. Lena had wanted a grand salon on the ground floor; Lutz and I knew that the Schloss, though it seemed to be generously dimensioned on the architectural ground plan, was actually better served by a long cosy living room centred on the fire. No Steinway. Indirect lighting. It was not the tinkling of Chopin nocturnes that would be the defining spirit of the house but the crackle of timber. So Lutz and I had subtly subverted Lena's ambitions, or rather aligned them to the realities of a B and B. Naturally, I had also told Lutz a little about my personal problems with Lena; that is what men do when they are engaged on some physical task. There is a limit to how much you can talk about Manchester United, especially with an Ossi ex-mariner.

Now I was worried that I had opened up too much to Lutz and that he might – as Harry seemed to suspect – have become a Fifth Columnist. Our usual crisis management chats had been replaced by silences punctuated by gruff enquires about Wayne Rooney's knee or ankle or groin.

One of the casualties of the Big Chill had been the Frog Emergency Plan. We knew it would bring chaos. We had even bought some cheerfully orange IKEA buckets to dump the frogs in. But we hadn't rehearsed the manoeuvre, we hadn't allocated our roles and we hadn't even talked about frogs for days even though it was our shared passion. That is what happens when trust between two men starts to evaporate.

Hence an event that we knew was about to happen took us by surprise. It was a bit like World War One in that respect. This much we knew: the frogs had to be scooped up using long-handled fishing nets, dropped into the buckets, carried to the pond and allowed to slip into the water. If we didn't carry that off they would be crushed by traffic.

Lutz went off in search of an ACHTUNG FROGS sign; I dragged Darren out of the kitchen and looked for the buckets.

Darren could barely control his enthusiasm.

'Frogs! Man, I love them! They're delicious!'

Outside, there was a green-brown multitude of writhing amphibians. It was as if the earth had come alive. A strange smell, not unpleasant, a little vinegary, as if one had caught the whiff of a fish and chip shop three streets away. And there was not – as one might have expected from a reptilian Love Parade – a mass, hysterical screeching but rather a dull, collective grunt. The frogs had been commuting miles and they were devoting their energy to flopping forward rather than sex-yodelling.

Five buckets, three nets, the kind kids use at the seaside to scoop up rock-crabs. We stood in the middle of a sea of 400 big brown frogs and in one scything movement tried to capture just two of them and sink them straight into a bucket. Not easy: frogs are jumpers and claustrophobics. Put them into a closed space and they will leap for freedom. 'True Ossi frogs,' grumbled Lutz as another two tried to escape captivity. The trick, we decided, was to put a sheet of newspaper over the bucket just as soon as it was half full. Even the most athletic frogs could not pierce the Motoring section of *The Sunday Times*. When a bucket contained fifteen frogs, Darren took it into the garden and emptied the females close to the warbling males in the pond. The rest was up to them. It was like the second plague imposed on Egypt to persuade Pharaoh to free the Israelites. When we were children, our Sunday school teacher used to read the passage from Exodus to us to show that nature was God's tool: 'The Nile will teem with frogs. They will come up into your palace and your bedroom and onto your bed, into the Houses of your officials and on your people, and into your ovens and kneading troughs.' While the rest of the class found the idea repulsive, I relished it: frogs in the bed, frogs in the kitchen! It seemed exciting, interesting, intriguing. I had wanted God to impose a plague on my home. And now my wish was coming true.

Swish. Scoop. Plop.

Swish. Scoop. Plop.

We developed a rhythm.

'It's like cutting down sugar cane, eh, Darren?' said Lutz.

'I come from London, Mr Lutz,' said Darren, a little breathless from the effort. 'We get our sugar from supermarkets.'

Lutz straightened up, without replying. He could hear a car engine.

'Quick,' he said, 'we've got to stop it!'

Easier said than done. How do you break free from a frog army that is covering not only your shoes but springing up to your knees, effectively pinning you down like Gulliver in Lilliput? We needed to cover some fifty yards across the green legions to reach the car. Darren showed the way by adopting a running stride, no doubt imitating some great Trinidadian hurdler, which involved throwing up legs in giant strides. Hanging on to our nets we loped our way towards the approaching vehicle. It was a heavily-laden four-wheel drive Mercedes and it was advancing at speed.

'HALT!' barked Lutz.

'Please stop!' I shouted.

'Put your fuckin' brakes on, man!' yelled Darren.

The car flew past us into the midst of the frog multitude, and suddenly cut its engines. The window was rolled down.

'What the hell is going on?' came a voice as rich as Dundee fruitcake. The door swung open. We saw a corduroy-trousered leg and an expensive brogue leather shoe descend tentatively from the car – and then withdraw quickly as Simon – for it was he – grasped that he was surrounded by hundreds of desperate frogs.

I edged closer to the car, scooping up a few amphibians on the way.

'How does it feel to be a frog-murderer, Simon?'

'I'll tell you how – it feels like I'm trapped in some bloody Alfred Hitchcock movie. Are they going to attack me?'

'Could be,' I said. 'Frogs as individuals are really nice. But if you start killing them in a systematic way, who knows? Maybe they're planning to get you as we speak.'

'Get inside and close the door,' said the Scotsman, with a sense of twitching urgency.

As I got in, Darren was inspecting Simon's tyres, which were plastered with amphibian corpses. There was nothing to be done for them: they were flat as postage stamps. Around about the tyres though there were dozens of dead, yet intact, frogs, killed perhaps by shock. Darren was moving around the car, picking up frogs and examining them scientifically.

I rolled down the window.

'What are you up to, Darren? You should be saving live frogs not performing autopsies.'

'I'm just thinking what I could do with their legs.'

Simon was nervous.

'Close the window! They could get in.' He rubbed his neck as if fearing vampire frogs. I couldn't understand Simon's terror – if he had been wearing a kilt there might have been reason for concern – but was quietly satisfied that at least something, even if it was just brown, tiny and slippery, could break through his wall of complacency.

'What are you doing here?' I asked in a somewhat strained manner. Simon's hysteria was infectious.

'Brought you some stuff.'

I glanced at his load.

'Sorry, didn't mean to snap. It's just that we weren't expecting you.'

'Lena rang to tell me you had problems with the pitch, so I thought I would help out.'

'Very sporting of you, Simon, thanks.' Thinking: Lena really is back in charge.

I should have called in help long ago. The pitch was a disgrace. You could train Ossis to play cricket but you couldn't reverse decades of Soviet environmental neglect in a couple of weeks.

We had held a second practice session with the village team the previous week and they were getting a rough idea of the game. Plus, Gundi had persuaded her ex-boyfriend Knut the Wrestler to take part. Gundi and Knut had once been a great romance, a 90-kilo Juliet and a 110-kilo Romeo. Knut was a few years older and when Gundi was being groomed as a teenager for possible swimming glory, he was already an established wrestler. Her coach didn't approve of the relationship but Gundi was not deterred. She bunked off from training sessions to accompany her lover to a Peace and Friendship wrestling championship in Varna. He was at his competition weight and so was given two seats on the Interflug flight to accommodate his bulk; she squeezed into the second and the plane seemed to tilt dangerously. Knut made her feel dainty. During the Varna adventure he plucked her up once and carried her out of the athletes canteen and, since the lift was broken, up seven floors to their hostel room. 'I'll do that again when we get married,' Knut had told her. But it was not to be: when they got back to the DDR, Gundi was reprimanded and Knut ordered to go back to his wife. Their love withered but Gundi would always say: 'You can count on Knut.' He was as big as Asia; no bowler could possibly spot the wicket behind his bulk. And he could hit the ball, sometimes.

So, we could produce a scratch team, yes, but the pitch was a mudbath, there was nowhere for spectators to sit and the whole atmosphere of the place was more Minsk than Manchester. Now Simon had come to the rescue, bringing a long roll of coconut matting, a kind of carpet that would stretch from one wicket to another. And in the back of the Mercedes I could make out a large field banner announcing 'FAIR PLAY FOR ALL!' A small tag on the banner declared that it had been Made in China.

'Simon, we can't just sit here as if we're in a Toad of Toad Hall traffic jam.'

'But what do you suggest we do?'

'We get out of the car – that's done enough damage to bio-diversity already – take the banner and use it to shovel up as many frogs as possible. Then we drop them in the pond.'

That is how FAIR PLAY saved the lives of hundreds of mating frogs and headed off a potential bloodbath. Darren's pile of frog corpses – victims, as he said, of 'friendly fire' – was nothing compared to what could have happened. Lutz pinned a huge ACHTUNG! placard on the back of the Mercedes so that other vehicles would slow down, and distributed some of Simon's red and white traffic accident cones around the vehicle.

I left Lutz and Darren to carry on scooping up the frogs and accompanied Simon back to the house.

'Sorry,' I said, not really meaning it, 'I didn't realise you were allergic to frogs.'

'Well, it's not something that usually crops up in conversation, is it?' grumbled Simon, smelling his hands. 'What is this stench?'

It was, of course, the special scent of frogs on heat but I wasn't going to share this knowledge with him. Perhaps I would wait until dinnertime.

'Time for a wash and brush up, I think,' I said, steering him toward the downstairs lavatory. 'We wouldn't want to inflict this on Lena, would we?'

'Good God, no.'

Simon locked the door and started to whistle some Scottish marching song. He evidently felt rather brave now that he was safely indoors.

Lena approached from behind and put her arm round my waist. She had become more tender since returning, as if she now understood at last that my work on the Schloss was not a way of dodging intimacy with her but rather an attempt at broadening it. I pecked her on the cheek and she barely flinched, ignoring the pungent frog perfume.

'I called Simon in to give the pitch a facelift,' said Lena, 'you don't mind, do you?'

'Course not.'

But, of course, I did. A bit. Now Lena was back in control of the house, the kitchen *and* the sporting activities. It seemed that we would never get the right balance: one of us had to be master and one of us had to be serf. The trick, Harry had told me, was to give Lena the *illusion* that she was the boss, while actually pulling the strings. 'Women have been up to that ever since Adam and Eve,' he said, 'you know, all that spare rib stuff? We have to play the same game otherwise we'll become the redundant gender.' As usual when Harry assumed his guru's guise, he lost me in the fog. But the fact remained: Lena was back, she was blooming, and harmony was returning to the house. As far as I was concerned, there were worse fates than that of Happy Serf.

Simon looked better for his wash and brush up.

'Excellent!' he boomed. 'That's better. Never seen the point of frogs, somehow.'

I raised my eyebrows but said nothing.

'Let's get the match details sorted out – only seven days before D-Day.'

'D-Day?' said Lena, puzzled. She had been off with a cold during the week that World War Two was taught in her school.

'D for Disaster,' I said, 'D for Depression, D for the Doldrums, D for Debts and Death.'

'D for Decisions!' said Simon and we let his enthusiasm sweep over us. My sense of the Cricket Match Day was that the game could only end in chaos. Therefore, our strategic focus should be the luncheon for the ambassador. If Lena and Darren could co-operate on that occasion then we could demonstrate to all and sundry – even the grudging ambassador and the unenthusiastic mayor – that the Schloss was a going concern. But Simon convinced us that the game too would be important. We could bring fun to East Germany; pioneer work. Making the Ossis loosen up, 'de-ossification' he called it, could be the Great British Mission.

Lena's eyes lit up as the Scot painted a picture of how Alt-Globnitz could, at least for a D-Day, be converted into the social hub of East Germany. He played the same ruse on me that Lena had tried when we first came to Alt-Globnitz in the winter: close your eyes and let your imagination unfurl. The colours, the noise. Tents for the press and the players, portable toilets painted in red, white and blue. A Highland bagpiper with hairy knees. He had high hopes that Richard Branson or some other entrepreneur could come up with a donated Wii cricket game. It was to be a Prussian carnival.

'I'm sure you will make the Schloss bloody magical for the occasion.' Lena blushed. Simon was a fraud but sometimes fake compliments were better than none at all.

'One thing you've got to remember,' he said, 'is that the Ossis have to win the game. If the English win, everyone here will say that it is a typical example of neo-colonialism. First we occupy a patch of land, then we teach the natives our customs and our games – then we beat them and thus prove that we have a superior civilisation and a moral right to rule.' Simon paused for breath. Sometimes he seemed to be rehearsing for the moment when he could take a seat in the House of Lords and nudge his honourable audience even deeper into a coma.

'But we don't do it that way anymore. FAIR PLAY is the slogan of the new Britain. And it means our moral superiority comes from letting the other side win! If the Ossis lose, the whole concept will collapse and so, I'm afraid, will the government funding for the Schloss. The Ossis need to feel like winners again – and when we let them win, they will love us.'

I thought about the team: Bernie who used baseball bats to win political arguments, Knut the Wrestler still dealing with the effects of steroid abuse, Peter the grenade-throwing bowler.

'Quite honestly, Simon, the Ossis would need a miracle to win.'

'Don't be such a wet blanket,' he said, 'life is full of little miracles.' As he spoke, I spotted a stray frog jumping across the living room, heading in his direction. I decided not to warn him until it entered his trouser leg.

Chapter 13

Napoleon and the Crapos

The sun started to shine again. It was June and it seemed as if the sun had taken a very long sabbatical. Wherever you went in Alt-Globnitz there were people angling their heads to catch the rays; you could observe the tension ease in their faces and, as muscles relaxed, the Alt-Globnitzers became young again. Colour returned and not just to their pasty features. For months Brandenburg had been a black-and-white landscape; suddenly the sky was Prussian blue and the trees were lush. Women swapped Pepe jeans for short denim skirts and did not mind that they had to swat mosquitoes on their bare legs. This was one of the few months when there wasn't a queue outside the sun-tanning studio. It was the moment when women got to show off the tattoos on their upper arms. Lutz went fishing off the jetty in the Globnitz lake and complained that it was crowded, meaning there were two other visible humans. He caught a carp and promised to take Harry and me out on a boat to catch eel. For over eight months, Wehrmacht-grey had been the dominant shade. Now grey had surrendered and lime-green was in occupation. Even the frogs, especially the frogs, noticed the difference. At two o'clock in the afternoon they were inert in the pond, like teenagers after clubbing all night.

A good day then for a cricket match.

Simon had been busy over the past fortnight, a more or less permanent guest in the Schloss. He had persuaded a building contractor to lend a digger truck and flatten at least part of the old Russian field. Some artificial lawn had been laid in the 18 metres between the wickets. It wasn't AstroTurf. It wasn't Lord's; it wasn't a glowing verdant green. But it was better than it had ever been before. Dog owners in Alt-Globnitz understood the change, abandoned the field and persuaded their hounds to shit on the pavement instead; it was the beginning, said Simon, of urban pride, the recovery of self-respect.

The question of cricketers wearing white had prompted a flicker of concern. Clearly, the English players already had their white flannel trousers and their white shirts and it would give them unfair advantage over the Ossi whose natural inclination was to wear a purple-blue training suit. But where, in the world of logos and neon-coloured T-shirts, was one to find immaculate white clothing? Lutz had a brainwave: hospitals. An old friend of his worked in a hospital laundry and was persuaded to loan out a dozen pairs of trousers – on condition they would be returned as soon as the match was over to prevent the spectacle of doctors with naked legs.

Fortunately Harry was back in Berlin and so there was no prospect of friction between him and Simon; being stuck in close quarters with the Scot for more than a week was becoming increasingly hard, even for someone like me with a reputation for tolerance. Once, engaged to rebrand a tinpot Asian dictatorship, Simon had driven to distraction a whole temple full of Buddhist monks; lifetime vows of patience and kind-heartedness and generosity to strangers were strained and discarded by the holy men after prolonged exposure to his very special type of Scottish arrogance. But I had to concede, Simon had organisational talent: somehow he had persuaded a PR company to fly in twenty journalists, experts on cultural diplomacy, to watch the game. A tent had been erected with space for a small safari table and five bottles of Scotch. A good-luck telegram had arrived from Simon's schoolmate, the prime minister, and while it wasn't exactly imaginative in its wording, it helped stir interest. 'ALL BEST WISHES FOR CRICKET SUMMIT, PM.'

'It's beautiful, like a fucking haiku,' said Harry when I read it to him over the phone. 'Seven words, notice. Rates get more expensive after eight words.'

Still, it had the effect of persuading a very reluctant ambassador to make the journey from Berlin. And to prompt the mayor to briefly abandon his scepticism about us; he would, said his secretary, be 'in attendance' – a phrase normally used by royalty – and would we please ensure a block of three seats since he would be bringing two guests.

Lena had been changing the Schloss around a bit and I could see it was truly becoming her space; the basement, dried out and painted a dazzling white, was now her work area. Although the original plan had been to share the office rooms, I could see that I would be confined upstairs, writing in the thankfully rat-free attic. The basement now had a sound system, a huge flat table – another one of Lutz's converted doors – flowers and light. The attic by contrast was still damp with a strange fetid smell, and it was impossible to ascend the wobbly ladder after consuming two small tumblers of whisky. An unequal division, perhaps, but the priority at the moment was to keep Lena happy. And she certainly looked happy, flustered but confident, as she made the dispositions for the match.

There would be a buffet lunch for the ambassador and the English cricket team. With ourselves and Simon, perhaps even Harry, that required catering for at least sixteen. Lutz and I hoisted the table to the centre of the salon while Lena and Darren prepared the food. Darren had, after a few rows, accepted the authority of Lena and, while he was the better instinctive cook – continually experimenting with tastes – he benefited from the discipline. Together they had dreamed up a culinary surprise and, as long as it didn't send the ambassador rushing to the toilet, I was ready to accept whatever they cooked. In fact a light case of food poisoning might actually be the only way that the Ossi Eleven could hope to beat the England Eleven.

The British players were healthy-living diplomats, hand-picked by the ambassador, and muscular security guards. A couple were in their mid forties but even they seemed to be fitness fanatics. Our spies told us that the team had been in training for the past month, with group jogging in the Tiergarten chanting like marines: 'One, two, three – vic-tor-y', and calorie-controlled lunches in the embassy canteen. All eleven had been banned from drinking gin and tonic or having sex in the seven days before the match. The order had come down from the ambassador, who was determined that the English side would smash the Ossis – and perhaps destroy our chances of getting more Schloss subsidy money from the British government.

Our team was still short of two players and I could see that problem was nothing compared to the poor physical condition of the Alt-Globnitzers. My solitary triumph as coach so far had been to persuade Peter the Plumber to take the cigarette out of his mouth before bowling the ball.

'We've been bonding fantastically,' said Adrian the English captain, who was officially registered in the Berlin Diplomats List as 'Second Secretary, World Trade Questions' and who probably worked for the secret service. 'How about your team?'

I thought back to the previous evening after our last practice. We had gone to Gundi's for a few beers and Toni, the ex-German army boy who was part of our Schloss work team, had got into a fight with Bernie, and we had all ended up in the Marktplatz at two o'clock in the morning in a huge shouting match. Bernie, in his cups, had complained that he was sick of being bossed around by a Scheissausländer, a bloody foreigner. Me. Why couldn't Germans be bossed around by Germans like in the old days? Toni said he was a fool. Bernie said Toni was a puppet. Toni hit Bernie. I just managed to stop Bernie clocking Toni with a bottle. We needed every skull intact for the match, irrespective of what was inside.

'Yeah, just fine,' I said, 'they're a finely oiled machine.'

The English team had arrived early, an hour before lunch – the ambassador was coming by Rolls Royce somewhat later – so that it could practise. The arrangement was that the team would stay in the Schloss overnight. The house was already beginning to feel crowded, people banging into each other as if they were rush-hour commuters on the Japanese underground.

'Where are we going to put everybody?' whispered Lena.

'We can put a few of them in camp beds in your office.'

'No,' said Lena, firmly. The basement was sacred ground. 'They can double up in the bedrooms. Most of them are probably gay anyway.'

I glanced at my watch. The sight of the Englishmen throwing balls at each other, as at a children's birthday party, made me think that I should be readying the Ossis for combat. It was eleven o'clock on a Saturday morning so most of them were probably still asleep or stumbling towards Gundi's for her special breakfast of blood sausage and fried eggs. But Lutz put paid to my plans.

'Can I have a word with you and Lena?' he asked, in a slightly funereal manner as if his dog had just died. Lena left Darren to slice up vegetables and we settled into a corner of the salon.

'I've just been talking to Doris, Doris Bonkerz that is. And I… we… thought you should know. Now that it's certain.'

I was impatient to get on with team training so I decided to hurry things along a bit.

'Let me guess, Lutz – you want to leave your wife and live with Doris.'

Lutz looked thunderstruck.

'Where did you get that crazy idea from?' he stood up, prepared, it seemed, to storm out.

'Yes,' Lena asked me, 'are you drunk?'

'Er, no,' I stammered. 'I just assumed. I just thought it was…'

'Sorry if there's been a misunderstanding,' said Lena to Lutz. 'Sit down now and tell us what's on your mind.'

'Yeah, sorry, Lutz,' I said. 'Sorry if I'm wrong.'

Lutz glared at me, and continued with his announcement.

'After the food poisoning thing I went to Doris to ask her how it could have happened and what the guests should be taking in terms of medicine. We got to talking and she said that Uwe had been in a few days earlier to get several packets of antibiotics. She wasn't really surprised because the mayor, who, you know, is a...'

'Hypochondriac,' I said, thinking of his antiseptic wipes.

'... just so, he often sent Uwe over to present prescriptions for medicine. This time though, Uwe asked Doris for a powdered or granulated version of the medicine. So when she heard about the poisoning she got all excited and started to look up in the Pharmaceutical List the possible side effects and cross-effects. Then she said to me: maybe it was the wine, not the food.'

'You mean Uwe put antibiotics into the wine carafes to make the guests sick?' asked Lena, aghast. She had found Uwe strange but not sinister and had never understood Lutz's mistrust. 'He deliberately tried to poison us?'

'Maybe just make you a bit sick,' said Lutz, 'it wasn't cyanide or anything. It's just that some antibiotics clash with wine. Anyway, we decided to check before we told you. So I found a glass that Darren hadn't washed up properly, with a bit of sediment in the bottom, and Doris sent it away for testing. The results are just in – all the symptoms, the dizziness, the abdominal pain, the vomiting, can be put down to a mix of the pills and the red wine.'

'Which is why Harry and I didn't get poisoned – we drank from our own bottle,' I said, 'and Darren didn't drink all night.'

'Uwe is a bastard, I always told you this,' said Lutz.

'Well, I don't want any violence,' said Lena. 'And I don't want anyone to do anything about it until after lunch.'

'I would say, we don't touch Uwe until the match is over,' I said.

'And the ambassador has left,' added Lutz who was still a little overawed that a man who had been knighted by the Queen was coming for lunch.

'But what are we going to do with him? Turn him over to the police?' I asked.

'Not talking about me, I hope,' boomed a familiar voice.

'Harry!' I said, pleased to see him after his two weeks in Berlin.

Lena was slightly less enthusiastic; she thought Harry exerted a bad influence on me, that our friendship was retarding my already slow progress towards adulthood. But she had come grudgingly to accept, since we started work on the Schloss, that Harry knew how to get things done. Even if his methods bordered on the criminal.

We passed on the information from Lutz.

'Aha,' he said after we had finished our exposé.

'Aha,' I said. 'Just one request, Harry – please don't arrange a car accident for Uwe until after the game.' We had to be sure that the British government kept on paying us to fly the flag in Brandenburg. And that ruled out attempted murder, at least for the time being.

'It also depends, as far as I remember, on you and your local boys winning the match,' said Harry. 'Seems to me you'd better get on with that. As for Uwe, I have a slightly different plan.' He pointed at his leather doctor's bag. 'It's all in here.'

'I'm not sure I like the sound of that,' said Lena.

Harry remained silent but a wide, beatific smile broke across his face. Just for a moment, he looked like the Dalai Lama.

Two hours to lunch, three and a half hours to the start of the game. It was time to check on the team. I was counting on the Schloss workers, in particular on Toni. He was probably the brightest on the team, not cunning like Uwe, and he was fit in the way German men used to be before they started going to fitness centres. That is – no muscles shaped like walnuts, just a man who was happy to be in the fresh air using his hands. So when Toni didn't answer the phone I knew something was wrong. His wife picked up and, before I had even begun to speak, launched into a long, detailed account of how poor Toni had been hit by the flu and how his temperature was so high, the mercury had almost shot out of the thermometer. I rang around. The other members of the Schloss work team had also supposedly been laid low; the description of their symptoms was identical and sure enough, mercury was shooting out of all of their thermometers.

'They're reading from a script,' said Harry. 'Someone's put pressure on them not to play. Just make sure the wrestler is coming. You need some hitting power.' I decided to make the call from Gundi's. If Knut saw Gundi's number on the display, he wouldn't dare to press the 'ignore' button. So I abandoned the increasingly hectic kitchen preparations, left Harry to brood over some documents in the salon, wended my way past the frighteningly competent English cricketers and made my way past the Café am Marktplatz – giving a cheery and rather relieved wave to Lutz's busy wife, looked through the window of the Sparkasse to see if I could spot Robert, and arrived at Gundi's feeling that Alt-Globnitz had become my kind of place. Not exactly home but familiar terrain.

Robert was propping up the bar and so was my old fellow Rolling Stone groupie Horst. They both grunted a greeting; Robert I could see was regretting the moment when he agreed to play the noble game. By way of a bribe I bought him an early morning Weizenbier. But it was Horst that I needed to recruit. We had trained the team together, Horst somehow transferring his knowledge of t'ai chi and karate to the gentle game of cricket; he was not, however, actually on the list to play. Now he was needed – we were embarrassingly short of players. I explained the situation.

'Those little bastards,' he said. 'Flu, my God.'

'So, will you play?'

Horst crumpled his face as if the beer had suddenly turned flat. I knew that he hated the idea of performing like a circus poodle in front of the ambassador, the mayor and assorted foreigners. He liked giving orders, in the way that volunteer workers often did, but he didn't like being just a humble member of a team. It was the rebel in him that gave me an idea.

'Mick used to play before he joined the band.'

'Mick?' Horst's eyes lit up.

'Yes,' I said, 'you know "Street Fighting Man"? It's about cricket.'

'You're not serious! I thought it was about...'

'Revolution, yes, people often make that mistake.'

'I suppose, I could play,' said Horst, chewing on the idea. 'But it's Knut you really need.'

Which reminded me: where was Knut? He was supposed to be driving from Neuruppin and should have arrived by now.

Gundi agreed to call him and was bombarded by a torrent of swear words from Knut. His car had apparently stalled. There was a smell of petrol, some smoke; an uneasy sense that the car was about to blow its top. So Knut had called the rescuing team of the motor association and they still hadn't arrived. It could take hours. Knut, in short, could miss the match.

'Tell him to get a cab,' I mouthed to Gundi.

This prompted more abuse over the phone from Knut.

'He says, do you have any idea what a fifty-five-year-old retired wrestler with a slipped disc gets paid in Brandenburg?'

Horst seized the phone from Gundi.

'Stop moaning,' shouted Horst, 'are you a man or a mouse. Honour is at stake!' Horst paused to allow the wrestler to make a bad-tempered reply. 'OK,' said Horst after a couple of minutes, 'I'll come and collect you myself.'

'That's good of you, Horst,' I said, although I knew it was an offer made out of desperation. If Knut played, Horst didn't have to. It was as simple as that.

'I'll get him there on time,' he said, downing his drink and leaving for the fire station. Emergency jobs called for emergency transport: it was a moment for the classic Horch fire engine, for flashing lights.

By the time I returned to the Schloss, the ambassador had arrived. We had hoisted the Union Jack on the flagpole and out of the attic windows fluttered Germany's Black-Red-Gold flag, the Brandenburg eagle and the European Union's blue ensign. Lena disapproved. All that cloth, she said, distracted from the façade, which was now scrubbed clean. I had overruled her – there was nothing like a bit of flag-kitsch to make a diplomat feel at home. The Schloss no longer resembled a broken-down hideout for junkies and drifters. The broken panes had been replaced, the window frames whitewashed; the roof plugged. You no longer risked breaking your ankle entering the front steps. There were so many tubs of flowers that Lutz had been sneezing allergically all morning.

The ambassador's Rolls Royce was parked in the drive and the chauffeur, standing guard to prevent it being stolen by Ossi gangsters, was watching Mac suspiciously. Dogs have a basic instinct to piss on luxury limousines but are also, in one of nature's mysteries, aware that chauffeurs often use their steel-tipped boots to protect their ground. Mac was casually smelling the wheels; the chauffeur calculating when to strike.

'Your boss inside?' I asked the chauffeur.

'Yes sir,' he said.

'My God,' I suddenly exclaimed, 'are those wood pigeons?' I pointed up at the blue sky.

The chauffeur peered, following my finger.

'Don't see nothing, sir,' said the driver.

'Nor me, not any more,' I said. 'A pity.'

Mac followed me into the house, looking at me, I like to think, with sneaking admiration at giving him the chance to piss on a Rolls Royce. There were not many West Highland terriers who could make that boast.

Inside, more flowers. Some kind of damp patch had suddenly appeared on the wall above the fireplace. We had nailed up an ornamental Afghan rug to cover it and if anything the hint of Orient improved the living room. There were a few nods to Prussia – in one corner we had positioned a walnut writing desk, which must have been used when the

Kaiser was running the show. Lena had found a modern lamp and placed it on top of the desk; Harry meanwhile had discovered an old World War One helmet, penetrated by a single bullet hole, in a junk shop and that too was on display. We had persuaded Lena that it could be used as an ashtray. Despite the bric-a-brac, the tall windows, the indirect lighting and the state-of-the-art kitchen gave the ground floor a very un-Prussian feel, a sense of openness. No hidden corners, none of that overpowering darkness that was so common in Prussian country houses. 'Great,' Harry had decided, 'no bloody antlers.' Lena's artful elongation of the room had the effect of making the ambassador seem even smaller than he really was. He had a Napoleonic stature. He even tucked his hand, in Bonaparte manner, inside his double-breasted blazer. Instead of a tie he wore a silk tuck-in cravat, a shirt with cufflinks, flannel trousers. Almost everything about him irritated me. I wasn't expecting to like him, and I wasn't disappointed.

'Ah, here you are,' he said, 'your charming, er, partner has been looking after me in your, er, absence.' A relieved Lena excused herself to go to the kitchen.

'Good trip?' I asked him.

'Yes, er, very interesting.' The slight hesitations injected into every sentence were, I realised, not intended as an ironic pause but formed part of a nervous tic. He seemed to be gulping for breath or perhaps to capture insects, like my beloved frogs.

'You must be pretty nervous,' I said, 'first time to the East.'

'Not so,' replied the diplomat. 'I have been to, er, Potsdam.'

'I think you'll find Potsdam is to the south-west of Berlin.'

'But you, er, know what I mean.'

'Not really,' I couldn't be bothered to be pleasant to the man since he plainly remained against the idea of the Schloss and saw anything east of Berlin's embassy as dangerous badlands.

The room was filling up. The England team had come in from playing with their balls and were washing their hands. Harry was there, still smiling. I recognised the warning signs: the twitching moustache, the rapid movement of his small eyes, the wolfishness – Harry was ready to pounce. But on whom? There was no mistaking the sense of mischief. He was virtually pawing the floor. Simon was chatting with the ambassador's secretary, a young rosy-cheeked woman with long coltish legs. I could see that she had not only the looks of a catwalk model, but also the conversation. I had wanted Knut to be there as part of my 'Shock and Awe' tactics – the same military technique that had been so successful in Iraq. There was nothing quite like a wrestler in the flesh to stop conversation at a genteel dining table. It looked though as if I would be denied this psychological weapon.

'By the way,' said the ambassador as we walked to the table, 'I believe you have hung the Union Jack the wrong way round.' I silently cursed the British flag which, with its many different red-white lines all with deep symbolic importance, was so difficult to get the right way up. The German flag was so much easier: Schwarz, symbolizing death, came on top, then Rot, signifying the shedding of blood, then Gold, meaning profit. All one had to do was remember some German history and it was easy to hang the flag.

I put Harry next to the ambassador since I couldn't face the prospect of an hour of small talk with Napoleon. Astonishingly Harry did not complain; he was on an inexplicable high even though it must have been clear to him, as it was to me, that our Ossi side did not stand a chance against the English, who had learned the game since they were first sent away to boarding school at the age of eight. And they were discreetly muscular; the kind of people who choose to run up the stairs of office buildings rather than use the lift.

The ambassador was keen to establish his authority from the very beginning, clicking his fingers to summon Darren.

'More wine over here please,' he snapped.

Darren paused wordlessly in front of the diplomat.

'Yes,' asked the ambassador, 'what's holding you up?'

'Just a question.'

'Fire away,' said the ambassador with a long theatrical sigh.

'Could I ask you what your last slave died of?'

Napoleon looked away abruptly and Darren plodded back to the kitchen, pulling up his cargo trousers and aware that everyone around the table had heard the exchange. When he returned, he came back not just with the requested wine but also with a big steaming bowl of frogs' legs, Darren's surprise dish.

'I thought we were trying to stamp out French eating habits in East Germany, not encourage people to eat this muck,' said the ambassador, no longer making any pretence at gracious behaviour.

'These are not French, they're East German, ain't they, sir?' said Darren looking over at Simon for support.

'They certainly are,' said Simon. 'Killed them myself.'

'And the recipe is from the Caribbean,' added Darren. 'We call frogs 'crapos' there.'

'It's a celebration of the multinational ingenuity of the British Commonwealth,' I chipped in. 'Rather brilliant.'

'Come on, Your Excellency, tuck in,' said Harry, already sucking the meat from the frog bones. The players enthusiastically joined in. The ambassador however pushed his plate away at the very moment that Harry chose to serve him four or five of the greasiest frog thighs. These promptly fell into the diplomatic lap.

'Oh well caught, sir!' said one of the cricketers. It was an innocent simple-minded joke, so the whole table felt free to laugh.

The ambassador however fumed. This was Napoleon, surely, looking defeat in the eye at the Battle of Nations, 1813. That, too, was fought in East Germany.

'Under usual circumstances,' he hissed, 'I would now leave and go home, pronouncing a curse on all your activities and your pathetic attempts to mimic British manners in this God-forsaken wasteland. But I will not forgo the pleasure of seeing your team of Ossis crushed at the hands of a team of English gentlemen.'

Harry pushed back his chair, stood up and clapped loudly.

'Great speech, Ambassador! Very strong!'

'Very nineteenth century,' I added. 'Refreshingly honest.'

I left lunch a little early, claiming that I wanted to get the Ossi Eleven limbered up for action. In fact, I had to check on numbers. It was clear that the team would now have to be propped up by Ossis-for-the-day.

'It doesn't add up,' I told Harry. 'Even if Knut turns up, even if I can persuade Horst to play, that's still only four with Robert and Peter the Plumber. There is Bernie the baseball-bat kid; that makes five even though he is a neo-Nazi. Then there is Simon; he's a Scot so he can be an honorary Ossi for the day...'

'The Ossis would do better without that windbag,' chipped in Harry.

'... makes six. Maybe Gundi can still find two more of her East German sporting mates.'

'Thank God they don't do drug tests before cricket.'

'And there's me. And there's you. We're one short.' The team was obviously going to be a mixed bunch of warriors, a sporting version of the French Foreign Legion. We had a common aim though: to cock a snook at the British Establishment.

'Me?' Harry was genuinely surprised, even though I had approached the issue with the subtlety of a blunderbuss. 'I can't play.'

'Do you think any of us can?'

'But it's a gentleman's sport – and I am not a gentleman.'

'True,' I said, 'you're a cheat and a liar. But that's what we need if we're going to win.'

'Well, OK, then,' said Harry, accepting the logic of my argument. 'But we have to bat first. I've got something to sort out and I can't be wasting my time standing around the field waiting for a bloody ball to fall from the sky.'

We had already bought in the beer for our batting period. The Ossis couldn't quite believe that half of a cricket match is spent hanging out on the boundary line, boozing and snoozing. The trick seemed to be to get two efficient batters to do all the work. If communism had taught them anything, it was this: delegate your two most active team members to sweat on behalf of the collective. The Ossi game strategy was thus – bat first, get pleasantly drunk, and hope for rain to stop play before they had to field.

'I'm not going to bowl,' Robert had told me after a training session. 'I don't like to run anywhere.' Since Robert had a say in a bank credit for the Schloss, I decided not to call him a lazy slob. 'OK,' I said. The question was, of course, whether we would win the toss. Harry said he had this in hand and I did not probe into this too deeply. Sometimes it was better not to know too much about Harry's plans.

'Looks like it's your lucky day,' said Harry as a bright red fire engine, blue lights flashing, came into view and halted with a squealing of brakes in front of us. Big Knut jumped out and I could almost hear the earth shake.

His whole body wobbled like a giant helping of panna cotta.

Knut caught my gaze.

'Relaxed muscle,' he said, grabbing one of the rolls of fat under his T-shirt.

'Very relaxed,' I said, 'it looks like muscle that has taken a year-long beach holiday.'

'Knut has persuaded me to play too,' said Horst. I slapped him on the back in gratitude and he flinched. The Brandenburgers needed time before they could easily accept physical contact. 'Lutz has got your whites – you can change behind his car.'

The cricket pitch seemed to me to have undergone a miraculous transformation. It looked plausible. The boundary of the pitch had been clearly marked by flags, some of them stolen Coca-Cola advertising banners; others little red Soviet banners, no bigger than handkerchiefs, that had been used in the old days to decorate the walls of the DDR-Soviet Friendship evenings. Two sets of six chairs had been 'liberated' from the Church. Lutz had picked the lock of the crypt and removed the plastic seats.

All in all, it was shaping up quite well. A small Scottish band had arrived – two bagpipes, a bass drum, a side drum, two fifes – and Simon was briefing them. They were being sponsored by a Scotch whisky company who had also taken on the task of supplying the press tent. I had a more or less full team, even if they looked, in their white trousers, more like bakers than cricketers; the sun was shining. The mayor's party arrived first. He seemed overdressed in a winter coat and black leather gloves, as if he had been tipped off about a sudden return of the Ice Age. He was flanked by the pinch-faced man I had seen him with in the central station in Berlin and a second man with tinted wide-framed glasses and a suit that was both lumpy and fashionable. Lena, radiant in cherry rather than Soviet red, ushered them to their seats. The village meanwhile was coming out in force: Gundi, rarely seen in daylight, had brought her own reinforced picnic-chair; she caught my eye and gave me a thumbs up to indicate that her former sporting buddies had arrived. Lutz's wife had briefly stopped working and Lutz himself was patrolling the boundary line. He had taken it on himself to act as security man, on the lookout for Uwe. The effect was of a German shepherd dog guarding its flock. Harry and I had agreed that Uwe had probably put pressure on the work team not to appear at the match. He might even have been behind Knut's car breakdown. In our current frame of mind, Uwe was the Devil incarnate, the Saboteur-in-Chief. Yet I couldn't figure out why he was going to all that bother.

At last, the British Ambassador glided towards the field, having driven the short distance in his purring Rolls. When he got out – or rather, descended like a seventeenth-century nobleman from his carriage – he glanced at the sky as if hoping for rain to wreck the occasion. At Simon's prompting, the Scottish band played 'Amazing Grace', a depressing song more suited to funerals. Lena went over to shake the ambassador's hand – not for the first time, I admired her poise, her ability to bottle up feelings and simply perform, acting on cue – and took him past the reporters' tent and to the mayor. They shook hands: the ambassador as if he were an astronaut on Mars greeting an alien; the mayor as if he had suddenly been exposed to the carrier of an exotic disease. The mayor's two guests stayed seated, staring straight ahead, and flicking ash from their cigarettes. I caught the whiff of an exotic tobacco.

Harry, meanwhile, had stepped into the reporters' tent and was passing round what was left of the grilled crapos.

'They're great, Harry,' said the Cultural Affairs correspondent from one of the British tabloids, 'they go really well with Scotch.'

'Everything goes well with Scotch,' replied Harry and there was a mumble of agreement. It was one of the few things that the British press corps could agree upon.

'What are they?' asked a cub reporter, obviously on her first foreign trip.

'Frogs' legs. Caribbean-style, cooked up by a brilliant young British chef.'

'You're kidding! In a dump like this?' This from the *Economist* reporter.

'Would I kid you? Could I kid you? The guy's being hailed as the new Jamie Oliver. Really cheeky fusion cooking – Trinidad British meets East German sausage meat.'

Harry promptly set up three interviews for Darren and was still negotiating photo rights when the band fell silent. There is nothing quite as satisfying as the moment when bagpipes stop playing. All at once what you imagined to be the beginnings of a migraine turns out to have an external cause and you feel that you are again in control of your brain and your ears. The thud-thud pulsing above your eyes fades away. You are healed.

The two teams ambled to the centre of the pitch: the English players with a bouncing step, counting on easy victory; the Ossis shuffling along as if in a chain gang. The umpire was a scholarly-looking forty-year-old, a member of a Berlin-based Anglo-German law firm. He was there because he owed Simon a favour.

'Who will call?' asked the umpire.

'I will,' said Knut and gave the umpire a euro.

The coin spun.

'Heads!' said Knut.

'Heads, it is,' said the umpire. Harry had reassured me before we walked out onto the field: he was in possession of a double-headed euro coin, minted by accident in Ireland, and it was brought out whenever he needed to guarantee a win.

'So we will bat,' said Knut, picking up the coin quickly. Knut was going to open the batting with Robert from the Sparkasse. Both were big men who could at least block the bowlers' view of the wicket.

The English bowler was a dangerous man, the embassy's expert on Anglo-German arms deals. He knew how to deliver a missile. The ball rocketed towards Knut who reacted too slowly. The ball just clipped off the bat, and had the English fielders been more alert they would have caught it, ending Knut's dreams of scoring a hundred runs in his first ever match. The second ball was equally fast, bounced off the ground and hit Knut's elbow. By the time the third ball came Knut was in a rage and without thinking slammed it out of the field – a six! The next ball suffered the same fate, getting similar treatment to that meted out by Knut to Jack the Avenger in a legendary wrestling match in Cologne in the early 1990s. Knut, in the DDR Olympic wrestling squad for the 1980 Moscow games, had become a trainer. But after the wall came down he went pro – and was pitted against an American with an Iroquois haircut whose speciality was to climb on the ropes of the ring and then jump on the spine of his prone opponent while letting out a Red Indian whoop. When Knut responded by throwing Jack the Avenger across the ring with one swipe of his arm, as big as a ham, he briefly became the hero of post-menopausal ladies throughout the Rhineland, the very heartland of wrestling fandom. Now he was putting in a repeat performance, this time with a cricket bat. Alt-Globnitz understood almost nothing about cricket but they could see that Knut was beating the hell out of the English. There were loud howls of approval from the villagers.

The British Ambassador sat with his mouth agape. Things were not going according to plan.

And the mayor too fidgeted nervously. This was not how the Alt-Globnitz tournament was supposed to go at all.

Something would have to be done.

Chapter 14

Howzat!

Knut was not, admittedly, the most graceful figure. There was something of Conan the Barbarian about him; Arnold Schwarzenegger smashing down a door and declaring 'Hasta la vista, Baby' seemed, by comparison, almost subtle. Knut saw the attraction of hitting a ball so hard that it flies out of the pitch, thus scoring six without actually having to run. And he was, in any case, an angry man. Cricket balls, cork wrapped in hard leather, made a pleasing impact. So it continued: THWACK! THWACK! THWACK!

The audience lapped it up. Gundi jumped up and down like a cheerleader.

'It's a good moment to strike,' said Harry, reaching into his briefcase.

'What do you mean?'

'Get Lena and I'll show you what I've got.'

I beckoned to Lena who seemed to be flirting with a Cultural Diplomacy expert in the press tent. For someone who had urged me to give up journalism as an essentially childish pursuit, she seemed to like their company. But then so did I.

Lena, Harry and I clustered at the far edge of the pitch. Lutz found some old Soviet ammunition boxes; Lena collected a plaid picnic blanket and laid it over the splintering wood so that we could sit down.

'This is it!' said Harry, like a stage magician who had just sawn his assistant in half. As if to say: you will never see anything more amazing than this.

At first, it was not much to look at. I was half expecting a pirate's map showing the place where treasure was buried.

Instead it was three loose typed pages, with blacked-out words and stamped BStU – extracts from a Stasi file. As far as I could make out it was the part of a dossier where a Stasi case officer outlined a brief biography of an informer and assessed his competence and reliability.

```
Informal Collaborator Codename Pille, born 16.
Feb. 1959, Karl-Marx-Stadt, member of Free German
Youth, studied chemistry university of Jena 1980,
research assistant Institute for Sport-Supporting
Pharmacology, specialism laboratory rat breeding,
Zuständigkeitsbereich Laborrattenzucht, performance-
enhancing pharmaceuticals for aquatic sports 1987,
member of the DDR delegation Olympics Seoul 1988.
```

Not exactly a fun read,' I said, returning the sheet to Harry.

'Now read this.'

```
Evaluation of IM Pille. Real name [blackened out]
```

```
IM Pille has shown himself to be an enthusiastic
and imaginative partner to the Ministry of State
Security. His direct work on preparing our team for
the Olympics had to be stopped because of various
skin allergies resulting from the laboratory work.
```

However IM Pille has proven indispensible in providing reports from foreign trips in which brother nations have exchanged information about pharmaceutically-supported training techniques. Trips have included Cuba (File Number HVA 403 bKu) and the USSR (File Number 3960 Sub 87). During his trip to the Moscow Institute for Sport engineering (Human division), IM Pille made contact with Andrej [Name blacked out] and Petr M [Name blacked out], visiting scholar from Sofia. It was agreed to set up an informal exchange network on latest developments in sport pharmaceutical research. (see: monitoring report HVA 7396 X Su 88). This co-operation continues and IM Pille is providing a regular flow of information. We see a promising future for IM Pille.

Signed: Schiller (Major)
8. Nov. 1988

'Don't you get it?' asked Harry impatiently.

'Oh, I do!' said Lena suddenly. 'This commie secret agent is the mayor. It all fits – his creepiness, his allergies...'

'His expertise with rats,' said Lutz who had been reading over our shoulders.

'But don't loads of people have Secret Police files?' I said. 'How's this going to change anything?'

'Patience,' said Harry, 'I've got tons of stuff on him. You see those shady characters sitting next to him. They're the Andrej and Petr named in the file.' He showed us two photocopied pictures. There was resemblance.

My bet is that they're still in business together – and they're up to no good.'

'Dirty business?' I asked.

'Obviously,' said Lena, who seemed to relish the prospect of a showdown.

'But can we prove anything?'

'You're behaving like a German again,' said Lena.

Interestingly enough, Germans themselves seemed to think that behaving like a German was tantamount to behaving like a wimp. What kind of mixed-up nation was that?

'Lena's right,' said Harry, 'Get a grip. This is not about legal niceties. It's about Shock and Awe.'

We walked round the pitch, Lutz tagging along in his new role as a human version of a faithful sheepdog. Knut was still battering the cricket ball. Simon was telling the journalists in the press tent exactly what they should write. The whisky bottles, I noticed, were virtually empty.

'So what are we going to do with all this Secret Police stuff?' I asked Lena.

'Embarrass the mayor and scare him away from the Schloss,' said Lena, 'but I don't know what Harry's got up his sleeve.'

To reach the mayor and the guests of honour we had to pass the press tent. Harry stopped and I assumed he just wanted to snatch a quick plastic beaker of Scotch. Instead he asked Simon to stand aside for a moment. He cleared his throat.

'Come on, Harry, have a drink,' said one of the reporters, 'it works wonders for dryness of the oesophagus.'

'My dear colleagues,' he said as if addressing the Roman Senate in the days of Cicero. 'Simon here has probably been giving you a lot of Public Relations crap about building relations between our two great nations, Britain and, er, Germany, that is, the mini-state of Ossiland. Well, you can forget all that.'

Simon turned pink.

'I'll give you the real story. Basically – come on, get your pens out! – the mayor of this charming little oasis in the Brandenburg desert is trying to stop a brave Anglo-German couple from restoring the Schloss – where you're all invited after the match for drinks and more of Darren's food – because he is in cahoots with the Russian mafia. He wants to take over the Schloss and turn it into a casino.'

'Not so fast, Harry,' complained one of the reporters.

'What do you want me to do – learn to stutter?' Harry, a dyed-in-the-wool reporter, did not hold his colleagues in great esteem. Most of them, he always told me, were good-hearted, slow-thinking people who would have been better positioned as attendants in a multi-storey car park.

'Where's the evidence, Harry?' This from the *Economist* reporter.

Harry reached inside his briefcase and took out a pile of folders.

'Lena,' he said, 'can you hand them out to these numbskulls.' They were the mayor's IM file, translated into English and photocopied and placed inside plastic folders so that they wouldn't be smeared by food.

'If you look carefully – and I'm addressing those of you who have not yet lost the ability to read – you'll see that IM Pille had contact with a Russian and a Bulgarian in the 1980s. That's those two gentlemen sitting over there, looking as if they would rather be casting for *Godfather Part V* than watching the British national sport.'

'I hope he's right about this,' whispered Lena. I liked the feel of her hot breath on my ear; her perfumed neck.

'Now the story is this – and you can confirm it with the captain of the English team, who is the top spy in the embassy, I'll give you his name later – is that Putin is cracking down on gambling in Russia. So people with money are looking for sympathetic places to play roulette. The Russian, the Bulgarian, the mayor, they've started a company to put a casino in Alt-Globnitz. In the Schloss.'

'How do you know that, Harry?' It was the fact-obsessed correspondent from *The Economist* again. He had plainly drunk less Scotch than everybody else.

'Because German bureaucrats are so much better than the British. If you apply for a gaming licence, you have to reveal everything, from the colour of your underpants to the name of the postman who had an affair with your mother. I've made some photocopies of the details.'

The reporters squinted at the gambling licence application. This had not been translated into English so most of the reporters squinted at it as if they were archaeologists examining a papyrus scroll.

'It gives the address of the casino as Schloss Alt-Globnitz, is that right?' asked one eagle-eyed reporter.

'No, it's not,' piped up Lena. 'I'm the owner of the Schloss.'

'And the mayor has been trying to sabotage our plans to turn it into an Anglo-East German cultural centre,' I added. 'He probably wanted us to do up the place, go bankrupt and then pick it up cheap.'

'Now,' said Harry, 'if you can still stand on your feet, I suggest you come with me for a little talk with the mayor.' Lena, wise to the ways, and the little weaknesses, of the British press, handed out Fisherman's Friend mints to the journalists to mask the smell of Scotch.

As they gathered up their laptop bags and tripped over the tent-ropes, there was a loud roar from the pitch. The ball had hit Knut's knee and he had sunk to the ground, like a wounded elephant hunted down for his tusks. Gundi and the villagers were screaming protests. I could see a small satisfied smile creep onto the face of the ambassador.

'Bloody buggering hell,' I said and left the press posse to run onto the pitch. The umpire looked worried. Knut howled. It was always difficult to tell with wrestlers how much could be put down to the Stanislavsky School of Method Acting and how much the body was in genuine revolt.

'He can't play on,' said the umpire and I agreed. We organised five of the Englishmen – one each for arms and legs and one to support the neck – to carry him off the pitch. Sweating and puffing, they transported the cursing carcass of the wrestler to the sideline, only to be assaulted by Gundi and her friends. Three of the English players returned limping to the match. 'A knee for a knee,' shouted Gundi at their retreating figures, 'that's what it says in the Bible.'

I put Bernie on instead of Knut, which was a bit like replacing Plácido Domingo with someone from *Pop Idol*, and the game resumed. The match, I could see, was now unwinnable; we would just have to be grateful if no blood was shed.

'Mr Mayor,' said Harry, 'I wonder if you could spare a moment for the ladies and gentlemen of the world press.'

The mayor looked up. I realised that he had swimmer's shoulders, broader and more muscular than the rest of his frame. Perhaps IM Pille had taken some of his own pills. His right leg was shaking but otherwise his body, his face, his posture gave no sign of panic.

'This is not the right moment,' said the mayor. 'We can hold a press conference about investment opportunities in Alt-Globnitz after the match.'

'Here's something you might like to discuss,' said Harry, handing over the IM Pille file. The mayor turned pale.

'And here's two for your friends,' giving one to Andrej (name blackened out) and one to Petr (name blackened out). 'Sorry I didn't have time to get a Russian and a Bulgarian translation.'

'Mr Mayor,' said the *Economist* reporter, 'why did you lie on your application for a gambling licence?'

'I'm not putting up with this!' said the mayor. He fiddled inside his jacket and for a moment I thought he was reaching for a pistol. Instead, he extracted a throat-spray and gunned it into his mouth.

'I mean, why did you give Schloss Alt-Globnitz as the site of your future casino when you don't own the Schloss?' *The Economist* was on the job.

'And what do your villagers think of turning an ancient monument into a money-laundering centre for the Russian mafia?' This from a tabloid reporter.

The mayor's two business colleagues rose wordlessly, grasping the files given to them by Harry.

'Wait!' called out the mayor. 'Let me just sort this out!'

But the two men did not reply and walked, at a sharp pace, towards a parked BMW.

Some of the reporters ran after them; most, rendered too tired and emotional by the sponsored alcohol, sat down in the seats surrounding the mayor and continued to pump him with questions.

After ten minutes the mayor pushed aside the *Daily Telegraph* ('Hey – watch it!') and the *Daily Mail* ('Bloody Kraut!') and made his exit. Once free of the pack, he wagged his finger at them furiously: 'You can prove nothing!'

'He's got a point, Harry,' I told him out of earshot of the reporters. 'We can't prove very much.'

'Yeah, I know,' he said, 'but it was good to shake him up a bit.'

There was a polite, almost childish cough, an 'a-hem', to our right. We turned to see the ambassador's glamorous personal assistant.

'Sorry to disturb you,' she said, 'but the ambassador was just curious as to what was happening.'

'Why can't he ask himself?' I asked, 'since he's only a few yards away.'

'Because then I would be out of a job,' said the woman, with a quick smile.

'Tell the ambassador we're going to take a short break in the game,' said Harry.

'That's a bit unorthodox,' I told him, 'in cricket you usually take a break after everybody has been bowled out.' That surely wouldn't take much longer: while we were quizzing the mayor, both Bernie and Peter the Plumber had been caught by the English fielders. Without Knut the team was falling apart.

'Just fix it with the umpire,' said Harry, 'slip him twenty euros. And get Darren to bring the ambassador some tea. I've got some business to do with Lutz and I can't do that if I'm standing on the field with a bloody stupid bat in my hands.'

The Ossi Eleven were happy for a break even though most had played for only a few minutes. Cigarettes were promptly lit up; Peter and Robert went to listen to the football results on the car radio. The Englishmen, aware that the ambassador was watching them with a hawk's eye, bounced up and down. I wondered if they did that in the embassy too when they heard his footsteps approaching.

'Hello Darren,' I said, as he approached me with an empty plate. He had offered the team slices of orange and lemon, the traditional half-time refreshment. The Ossis, suspicious of vitamins, had waved them away but the English killer-team had simply taken double portions. 'Try not to spill hot tea on the ambassador.'

'I made sure it was lukewarm, man, no harm done,' said Darren. 'But I want to ask a favour.'

'Fire away,' I told him, 'but it better not involve money. I just spent my last cash bribing the umpire.'

'No worries. I just want a chance to play.'

'You, Darren? I thought you were more into, you know, urban pursuits. Running away from policemen, knife-throwing, that kind of thing. Not exactly the Olympic disciplines.'

'Cricket ain't an Olympic game.'

'True. Sad, but true.'

'We in the West Indies, we've got cricket in our blood.'

'That must be uncomfortable.'

'We've had really good players. Viv Richards for example.'

Viv Richards was indeed a brilliant cricketer. His nickname was Master Blaster because of the force with which he used to hit the ball. And he was certainly from the West Indies.

'OK,' I told Darren, 'you can go on after the break. Ask Lutz to get you some white clothes.'

Lena strolled up and put her arm around Darren's shoulders. I was pleased that they were getting on: there was nothing quite as unifying as shared distaste for an unappetising British diplomat. Even one of the embassy team had come up and whispered an apology for his boss. 'Sorry, old man, just thank your lucky stars that you don't have to work for him.'

Darren scurried off in search of Lutz, almost slavering with excitement at the prospect of hitting a ball.

'Are you starting to understand the game?' I asked Lena. We were at ease with each other again but there was still a slight formality to our conversation, a sense of caution. She had run off; I had lost face with Harry and Co. Now she was back and I couldn't completely pretend that no porcelain had been broken. I wished that she could put her arm around me as she had just done with Darren. Sometimes the Trinidadians got all the lucky breaks.

'Sure,' she said, 'what's not to understand? Why do the English think that everything they do is so complex and sophisticated that foreigners are always baffled?'

'Just a question,' I said. 'A polite question.'

'Sorry,' she said, 'that lunch was a bit of a strain.'

'Very nice though. You pulled it off.'

Lena smiled.

'Isn't there a rule about the weather in this stupid game of yours?'

'Yeah. Rain stops play.'

Lena looked upwards. The sun was being blotted out by a cloud as black as coal.

We smiled at each other.

'Are you thinking what I'm thinking?'

'Yup,' I replied, 'God is a Prussian, not an Englishman.'

'An Ossi-God,' nodded Lena. 'You can always count on him to make it rain.'

The game resumed. Darren looked ridiculous. His borrowed white trousers were made for someone twice his size – an obese surgeon perhaps – and had to be held up with a knotted piece of string that Lena had found in the medical chest of Horst's fire engine. Soon he established a rhythm. Watch the ball soar towards him, thump it up high towards the upper levels of the Soviet barracks, then re-tie the knot of the rope around his waist. It worked very well. I dimly remembered Viv Richards performing in my youth, humiliating England with astronomic scores like 126 runs or even, on one occasion, 291. That was in the 1970s when all young over-educated red-blooded Englishmen wanted England to lose against its former colonies; anything else would have aligned us with the imperialist plutocratic exploiting class. Times had changed of course. Still, there was something perversely satisfying in seeing Darren, the offspring of an immigrant, helping the Ossis to victory over an English team supported by a bigoted post-colonialist ambassador. THWACK. Pull trousers up. THWACK. And the clouds were turning a satisfying dark blue.

'Come with me,' said Harry creeping up behind me. 'Now!'

I left the pitch reluctantly; studying the changing colours of the ambassador's cheeks had been a fascinating exercise. Once out of view of the spectators, shielded by bushes and trees, Harry made me run head down as if avoiding sniper fire. Within seconds we had reached Lena's Opel. Lutz was standing by the car, tapping his fingers on the roof.

'She lent us the keys,' said Harry without me having to ask. 'Open up, Lutz.'

Inside was Uwe, lying on his side, trussed like a turkey.

'One word and I'll put masking tape on your mouth,' said Lutz.

In the distance, I heard THWACK! and another ripple of Ossi applause.

'Uwe has confessed,' said Harry, 'haven't you, Uwe?'

Uwe's eyes were preternaturally big, full of alarm.

Harry banged the side of the car.

'Haven't you, Uwe?'

'Yes.' He didn't sound too certain.

'To what?'

'To working together with my brother-in-law…'

'The mayor,' interjected Lutz.

'The mayor,' continued Uwe, 'to sabotage the renovation of the Schloss.'

'You see,' said Harry, 'a confession and we didn't need to push his head under water or deprive him of sleep, all that American torture stuff, did we Lutz?'

Lutz shook his head. He was plainly enjoying the moment.

'No, all we needed to do,' said Harry, 'was to appeal to the power of reason.'

'The power of reason,' affirmed Lutz.

'Which functions best when the head is held upside down,' said Harry, 'that's what scientists say. I googled it. All the blood flows to the brain. It's the most logical position for a human.

So we hung him up for a while. It's a bit like yoga, isn't it, Uwe?'

Uwe was silent.

'You can't do this,' I said.

'Why not, it's easy,' said Harry. 'All you need is a bit of rope, a hook, a blindfold, and twenty to thirty minutes of free time.'

'No, I mean you can't do it morally.'

'Oh,' said Harry. 'Morally.' He pronounced it as if it were a foreign word encountered while flicking through a dictionary. Uwe was struggling with his ropes.

'But we are friends, Uwe and I, isn't that so?' Harry lowered his face into the car back so that he was within a few centimetres of Uwe's nose.

'Yes, Harry.'

'That's it, Uwe. We'll need you to have a little chat with a policeman just as soon as we've won the match.'

Harry raised his head. He had caught the sound of wood on leather, followed by clapping.

'Who's batting?'

'Darren,' I said.

'Ah, that's my nephew!' he said, almost giddy with pride. 'Family, eh, Uwe,' oozed Harry, looking into the car back. 'You can't beat it.'

'Yes, Harry,' said Uwe, 'that's right.'

And Lutz cut him free.

It was starting to spot with rain. My calculation was: another ten runs before the skies opened would give us at least a moral victory. If it turned out to be a mere summer shower and the English came in to bat, they wouldn't have time to match our score. But if it rained past teatime, the game would be scrapped and all that would remain would be the memory of Ossi batting powers. Darren was still at the wicket. Unlike Knut, he was hitting the ball with a natural, almost lazy grace.

Darren spotted that his uncle was back on the field. There was something about the slope of his shoulders that told me he wanted to impress Harry with the next shot. I told Harry to stop talking on his mobile phone and pay attention. This time the bowler was one of the embassy security guards. They were selected for their job – turning away inconvenient visitors – because of the breadth of their chests rather than the depth of their intellects. It was natural for them to feel a certain frustration. After all, neither men nor women wanted to be recruited on the basis of anatomical measurement. Some of that pent-up anger was on display as the guard plodded up to the line like a hefty carthorse and threw his round missile at Darren. Faced with similar levels of hostility in everyday life, Darren would normally accuse his assailant of racism (even if his assailant was black, because there was nothing worse, he once told me, than a black-on-black racism). But when an angry man is hurling a ball at 100 kph toward you, you don't argue. You either duck, throw yourself on the ground like Bernie, or make sure that your bat connects.

Darren scooped the ball up with his bat and sent it flying upwards. It took so long to reach its zenith that the English diplomats had time to peer up and follow its trajectory.

'Look out, Ambassador! It's heading for you!' But His Excellency, realising that the game wasn't going his way, had lost all interest in the game and was dictating a letter to his personal assistant. By the time he looked up, it was too late.

The ball came crashing down on a lap that had already made contact this afternoon with sticky frogs legs and with milky tea. So far, though, the damage had been done only to his pride and to his trousers; an ample ego would rectify the former, while the British taxpayer would no doubt pay a dry cleaner to take care of the latter. But this attack was altogether more intimate and it was difficult to see how even the long-suffering British taxpayer would be able to restore the damage.

'Aaaaaaagghuuuugh!' groaned the ambassador.

The personal assistant, unaware of the cause of the diplomat's discomfort, struggled to put the word into shorthand on her notepad.

The ambassador jumped up to his full Napoleonic height and I could only hope for his sake that his private parts were also of Bonapartian scale.

'Right on target!' said Harry, as the ambassador limped towards his Rolls Royce, one arm over the shoulder of his personal assistant, the other cupping the damaged zone.

'The Ambassador has just remembered a previous engagement,' called out the personal assistant to Lena. 'So sorry, must go!'

'Shall I bring you some ice?' asked Lena, thinking no doubt of the bucket in the press tent. Some reporters preferred their whisky on the rocks.

'No, there's plenty in the Rolls.'

Within minutes Darren had scored a few more runs – and the Ossi Eleven looked as if they could pull it off. A triumph for Fair Play and Bad Weather, even if the climax was sadly not witnessed by either the mayor of Alt-Globnitz nor the British Ambassador to Germany.

What had happened to the mayor? Lutz's wife, spying through the window of her café, had seen the mayor and his secretary carrying cardboard boxes full of files and loading them into the back of a van. It seemed like a total evacuation. Even the cactus was on the pile. The mayor could be seen yelling into his mobile. 'If there had been helicopters it would have been like the Americans getting out of Saigon,' said Harry, who had gone round to watch the sudden retreat. 'I've never seen anyone with so much panic written on his face.'

Our bet was that the mayor's friendship with his Russian and Bulgarian investors was now looking very wobbly indeed. So shaky in fact that he would have to change his address on a regular basis for the next year or two. Shady casino operators cannot take too much sunlight.

'He's got to go undercover,' said Harry, 'where do you think he's gone?'

'St Helena,' I said, thinking of Napoleon's last place of exile, a remote island in the Atlantic.

'Iceland,' said Lutz, who had once got drunk in Reykjavik harbour.

'Somewhere in the Sahara,' said Lena, 'he'll set up a Brandenburg theme park in the sand.'

'Nah,' said Harry, 'he'll go to some bolt-hole in Wales, you mark my words. Everybody disappears in Wales.'

Word of the mayor's flight spread through Alt-Globnitz and although the place had been left without a leader, there was a sense of liberation, of carnival. The Ossis, I realised, would always hate their leaders. Those decades of subservience to plump Politburo chumps in bad suits had wrecked their trust in leadership. It didn't matter who you put in charge, J. F. Kennedy or Mother Teresa, they would always rejoice at their going. For now, but probably not for long, Schloss Alt-Globnitz was the place to be, the counterweight to a Rathaus that was drawing down the shutters.

Villagers collected their umbrellas and crowded in the garden of the Schloss that evening and the cricket-victory party began to feel like a revolutionary event. It was one of those where-were-you-when moments that get etched into historical memory: Princess Diana's wedding, the fall of the Berlin Wall, the moment when Gordon Brown called a pensioner a bigot.

'Better go out on the balcony and give a speech,' said Harry. 'Wave a bit, like the Queen.'

I ignored Harry. That was going to be my next New Year's Resolution: ignore Harry more.

Inside, there was plenty to do as two cricket teams, a gaggle of hacks, a bagpiper and half a village squeezed into the ground floor, turning what had been a tastefully decorated salon into a crowd scene from a Cecil B. DeMille film set. It was noisy, it was smelly (too many men) and, with the help of enough Aldi wine to fill the Channel, it was well lubricated. If the Stasi Secret Police had sent along an undercover agent, he would have noted that:

The English cricketers, relieved that they were no longer under the scrutiny of the ambassador, let themselves go.

The MI6 spy danced with Gundi.

Simon, denied the presence of the ambassador's personal assistant, turned his attention to Lena.

Lutz discussed torture techniques with the British defence attaché, leaving occasionally to feed one of Darren's canapés to Uwe, who had been tied up once again, this time to a tree near the frog pond.

Darren taught darts to Robert the Sparkasse manager.

Mac tried to make love to a set of bagpipes.

Bernie came to apologise for writing 'Foreigners go home' on the wall of the Schloss and said he was going to apply for British citizenship.

Knut, limping on a stick, discussed the three best ways of breaking a man's neck with the *Economist* reporter.

Doris Bonkerz popped by to make sure no one was being poisoned and smiled at Lutz.

Harry opened a bottle of wine.

Harry opened another bottle of wine.

One of the English diplomats did a handstand to impress Lena, lost his balance and broke the pigskin of a Scottish drum.

Toni and the other workers dropped by to apologise for not playing in the match – Uwe had threatened them with the sack if they took part.

Doris revealed that the mayor had kept rats in a big wooden doll's house in his garden and spent his free time trying to train them.

Mac bit Bernie's right arm.

Simon said that after he had finished rebranding Brandenburg, he would be travelling to North Korea to discuss how to make the place more fun.

The ambassador's personal assistant rang to say that the Rolls Royce had broken down for the first time in the history of Rolls Royces. Could someone from the embassy come to help?

Horst got into his fire engine to rescue the ambassador.

Simon took his Mercedes to rescue the personal assistant.

Knut kissed Gundi.

Lutz climbed on to the table to deliver the speech he would make if he were elected mayor.

He promised to make Alt-Globnitz the Frog Capital of Germany.

The table collapsed.

Darren served fish and chips to the villagers in the garden.

The rain stopped.

The party moved outside.

Later, after we had packed everyone into bed, Harry, Lena and I sat in the far corner of the salon, away from the debris of the party. None of us was drunk, not even Harry, and we sipped tea with a hint of ginger.

'I feel sorry for the ambassador,' mused Harry, 'getting hit with Darren's ball.'

'Don't feel sorry,' said Lena, 'I didn't get the feeling that it was a particularly active part of his anatomy.'

'I mean, it's really painful,' continued Harry regardless, 'I was hit by a cricket ball once, on the head. Walking along past the Oval cricket ground in London, I was, suddenly this bloody ball flies over the wall and smacks me in the back of my skull. I've still got the scar.'

'A message from God,' I said.

'A warning,' agreed Lena.

'Yeah, well, I was knocked unconscious and it was like they say about people who are about to die – all my life started to flash before my eyes. The first pub I ever went to when I was sixteen or seventeen, not much younger than Darren – El Vino's wine bar in Fleet Street, where I learned the art of imaginative reporting; the cocktails at Chicago Matchbox; the Queen Victoria bar where I went for a few drinks immediately after getting married. It all went by – just like that – and then I recovered consciousness. Bloody cricket.'

'I didn't know you were married,' said Lena.

'Don't remember much about it to be honest,' said Harry.

'Strange,' said Lena, turning to me, 'I thought you were married to Harry.' I raised my eyebrows at Lena's little joke.

'It's true enough,' said Harry. 'We can't live without each other. In fact I'm thinking of moving down here, saw a nice barn that I could buy. Then I could come round all the time.'

'Yes, Lena would like that,' I said.

'We could grow old together, all three of us,' said Harry. 'I've worked out the finances. If I take late retirement and die early, I've got about enough saved up.'

I nodded.

'We could play golf together.'

'And put on those stupid jumpers that they always wear.'

'Great game, golf,' I said.

Lena was silent for a while. 'You're making fun out of me, right?' she asked uncertainly.

It was our turn to keep our mouths shut.

'Come on, Harry, you can't be serious. It would drive me crazy if you lived next door. You are chaos incarnate. As for golf...' Lena shook her head. We had put forward a terrifying dystopian vision of the future.

Harry sighed, then reached forward and gave Lena a loud kiss on her cheek.

'Of course we're bloody joking Lena. Do you think I want to sit around here and watch this guy go cold turkey off journalism?'

'That's good,' said Lena, 'because I've also got an announcement about the future – I'm pregnant.'

I felt as if I had been run down by a bus. Or hit by a cricket ball.

'Great!' said Harry slapping his knees, 'you can have your own little squawking, bed-wetting Ossi.'

I got up to hug Lena. 'Yes, it's fantastic, darling,' I said. And thought: Yes, it feels right.

'Now we have our third heart,' said Lena, letting herself smile.

And, of course, Harry took charge.

'Right, what are we going to call him? Erich?'

'A William. Or maybe Wilhelm,' I suggested. Thinking: if the House of Windsor can muddle up German and English genes, so can I.

'I prefer Erich,' said Harry, searching in the kitchen for champagne. All he could find was Rotkäppchen, the cheap East German bubbly.

Lena stood up, took three glasses out of the cupboard and waited for Harry to open the bottle.

'I've got news for both of you. It's a girl. And I get to choose the name. From now on, the women are in charge.'

A YEAR IN THE SCHEISSE
Getting to Know the Germans

Roger Boyes

£8.99

ISBN: 978-1-84024-648-3

Paperback

'We don't want you selling your body. Or even body parts. Even if you sold a kidney you would be lucky to fetch €5,000, and that, quite frankly, wouldn't really solve anything at all. Apart from being illegal, I mean. What I had in mind was you selling your soul.'

This is the story of an English journalist's absurd adventures living in Germany. Facing bankruptcy, Roger is advised by his accountant to make use of a legal loophole: in Germany married couples have their tax bill halved. So the search is on for a bride. Meanwhile his father, a former war hero, is also in financial trouble and is threatening to move to Germany and sponge off his son. The combination of crises sets in motion a hilarious romp during which we discover more than we really wanted to about German nudist beaches, the British media's obsession with Adolf Hitler and how to cheat at the Berlin marathon.

'I scheissed myself laughing. Herr Boyes has written a thigh-slapper of a book'

Henning Wehn, the German Comedy Ambassador